Pygmy Goats.

Pygmy Goats As Pets: A Complete Guide For Pygmy Goats Owners

By

Edward Dunbarn

GW00566978

Table of Contents

Introduction

A Pygmy Goat is a miniature goat breed that originated from West Africa. As they were commonly found in the Cameroon Valley they were once known as the Cameroon Dwarf Goat.

These animals can be used for milk production but are most commonly kept as pets. Their small size coupled with the fact that they can adapt to virtually all climates and are fairly hardy creatures mean they make ideal companions.

It is worth noting that in the UK there used to be two types of miniature goats; one which was bred for milk; the Nigerian Dwarf Goat and one which was bred for meat; the Pygmy Goat. At some point these two breeds were interbred and they are now all classified as Pygmy Goats. Whilst there might be some similarities and the two can look alike to the novice goat enthusiast, there are also some differences.

This book will focus primarily on Pygmy Goats.

Chapter 1: The Pygmy Goat

Definitions

Kid – A baby goat. May also be referred to as a Buckling (male) and Doeling (female)
Nanny or Doe – A female
Buck – A male
Wether – A neutered male

As one of the smallest breeds of goats these animals are often mixed up with the Nigerian Dwarf Goat but there are differences with regards to their size and features.

Size
A fully grown female Pygmy Goat will weigh about 53-75lbs (approximately 24-34 kg) and can measure around 16-23 inches (approximately 40-58cm) tall. Males can weigh between 60-86lbs (27-39 kg) and can measure around 16-24 inches (approximately 40-61cm) tall.

You may hear people talk about measuring their goats' height "at the withers" which simply means the shoulder blades, as this is the tallest point.

Whilst they may be small in height, Pygmy Goats can get fairly heavy, which means they can often look chubby, as they get older.

This shouldn't be a concern unless they become so overweight that it affects their health.

Coat And Colours
A Pygmy Goat's coat should be straight with medium length hair, although this often changes in density with the seasons.

Their colours and markings can vary but usually fall into the category of black, agouti or caramel and within each of these groups the coat could have different coloured markings.

Features
The head of a Pygmy Goat is slightly concave with a rounded muzzle. Their ears should be of medium length, firm and stand erect.

Their eyes are brown in colour, bright and prominent without being protruding. Pygmy Goats should NOT have blue eyes and this could be an indicator of genes from a different breed such as Nigerian Dwarf Goat. Although this shouldn't be an issue if you are just looking for a pet, you won't be able to register or enter them in shows because they won't be classed as pure blooded animals. Secondly, it is always better to know the ancestry of your goats so you can be reassured that they are healthy and aren't going to be prone to any serious medical issues further down the line.

Pygmy Goats are born with horns but you can have these removed and still enter them into shows.

A male Pygmy Goat may have a long and full beard whilst a female may have a very sparse beard or may not have a beard at all.

Lifespan
A Pygmy Goat that is properly cared for can live on average ten years, although it is not unknown for them to live up to fifteen years. This means they are a fairly long-term commitment.

Which Should I Choose?
When choosing a goat you may be wondering whether you should choose a male or female or if you should go for a younger goat

rather than an older one. As with anything there are advantages and disadvantages to all.

If you are a first time goat owner it is recommended that you start with an adult or late adolescent as they are easier to care for than babies.

If you want to milk your goat then of course you are going to need a female – either one that is pregnant or who has recently given birth.

Does, or wethers, are the best goats to keep as pets because they tend to be more docile, friendly and content amongst their own herd. Wethers tend to be less aggressive than does but are at higher risk of developing kidney or bladder stones which could result in costly vet bills.

Intact males tend to be more aggressive and harder to handle. If you are an experienced goat farmer that is regularly breeding several females then keeping a male goat on your property makes sense but if you are just looking for a pet then an unneutered male is not recommended. Of course all animals are different so one buck may not act in the same way as another but it would be wise to err on the side of caution just in case, especially if you have children living on or regularly visiting your property.

The other case against bucks is that they have some disgusting and annoying habits when they are in rut. Not only do they become very aggressive but they are also very smelly. To attract a female they will urinate on their front legs and faces which leads to their faces and beards becoming crusty over time which makes them very unpleasant to pet or handle.

One Goat Or Two?
Even though you may think you have all the time in the world to spend with your new pet, these animals are herd animals by nature and unfortunately need companionship of their own kind. No matter how much affection you give them and how much time you spend with them they will not be happy unless they have at least one other Pygmy Goat as company. This means you need to keep at least two goats or more in order for them to thrive. A lone goat will become

7

stressed and unhappy which in turn can lead to serious health conditions.

You may be thinking, great, an excuse to buy more of these beautiful animals but think of the practicalities; two goats mean you need more space, more food, more money as well as the time and attention to care for them. If you bought two and one of them died then you would need to replace it rather than leave the remaining goat by itself. This means that owning goats is a big commitment.

Whilst goats can live comfortably with other animals it is not recommended to keep them with dogs. Some people do claim to keep their goat with a dog with no problems but some dogs see these tiny creatures as prey. Sometimes a goat's playfulness ignites a hunting instinct in a dog which causes them to chase and hunt the goat which can, more often than not, end in disaster.

Be very cautious when introducing a goat to other animals as, like people, they all have different personalities and may not always take to each other. The difference between goats and people however is that whilst people will just avoid anyone they don't like, a goat taking a dislike to another animal can end in injury or death for your goat.

Do Pygmy Goats Make Good Pets?
YES!
These goats are so adorable that you cannot help to fall in love with them immediately. Personality wise they can be aloof yet they are

friendly and incredibly playful. Females tend to have a gentler and friendlier disposition whereas bucks can have a bit of a stubborn streak and are more independent and headstrong but generally speaking either sex are fairly good natured.

They love being lavished with attention and if you show them love and affection they will respond lovingly which, in my view, makes them the perfect pet!

It may come as a surprise but you can actually train Pygmy Goats to do all kinds of tricks which can be lots of fun, especially if you have children. You could spend hours just watching them running and jumping about and interacting with each other. They really are a joy to keep.

Their laid back nature and small stature makes them great service animals for nursing homes and hospitals.

These goats are fairly hardy creatures and can adapt to all climates and all seasons given the proper care and housing which means as long as you understand their needs and how to meet them they can be pretty easy to keep as pets.

They love sheep but can live comfortably with other livestock such as horses, llamas, donkeys, cows and so on which makes them a great addition to a small farm or animal rescue centre.

An added bonus is that Pygmy Goats can produce a lot of milk for their size which is great should you want to have your own fresh milk supply. Many people will say that goat's milk tastes a lot nicer than cow's milk and those that have an allergy or intolerance to cow's milk find that they can actually drink goat's milk without any issue.

Compared to bigger breeds of goats, a Pygmy Goat won't eat as much and as they aren't as tall you shouldn't require such a high fence that your back garden resembles an enclosed prison exercise yard. Their size also makes them easy to transport should you need to take them to a vet or if you intend to enter them into shows, as often they will fit comfortably into a large dog crate.

Of course, the question I answered was "do Pygmy Goats make good pets?" A better question to ask might be "is a Pygmy Goat right for me?"

The answer to the latter depends on what you are looking for in a pet. If you want one that you can keep indoors and snuggle up to whilst watching the television then these probably aren't the pet for you. Despite what some people will say these are very much an outdoor kind of pet and even though you may see lots of pictures on the Internet of cute little goats sat on people's sofas or cuddled up on the bed, keeping them inside is just cruel.

There is a downside to Pygmy Goats; despite their tiny appearance they do need to have a fair amount of space to run about and they will need lots of toys to keep them occupied. Whilst it hasn't been scientifically proven that these animals are claustrophobic they really don't like enclosed spaces so if you have visions of keeping them in a dog kennel or cage in a tiny back garden then think again. These animals are very clever and will get bored very easily. They are also very athletic and need to be able to exercise.

Another drawback for some people is that you have to have at least two of these animals in order for them to be happy.

If you do intend to buy a Pygmy Goat then you will need to be prepared to commit to them for the long-term which means you should consider what you will do with them should you wish to have a weekend break or a longer holiday. Whilst you can easily board a dog in kennels it may be far more difficult to find a carer for a goat.

As long as the Pygmy Goat suits your home and lifestyle then they can pretty much do what other pets such as cats and dogs do in terms of petting, playing and interacting with humans but with a more unusual, exotic element.

Cost

Whilst I usually like to give a complete breakdown of how much keeping a certain type of pet will cost the price of Pygmy Goats in terms of purchasing and keeping them is very dependent upon the type of goat you buy and whether you purchase everything new or whether you recycle or repurpose items or even source them for free.

Are you going to buy a registered goat or an unregistered goat? If you are buying a pet that you are never going to breed or show then there is no reason why you can't go for one that is unregistered. If you want Pygmy Goats that you can breed or that are of high show quality or milking standard then you may want to pay a bit more for them. Just be aware that if you do buy unregistered goats then you may find it harder to re-home them if you found that you needed to do so at a later date for whatever reason.

The next decision you have to make is whether you want a doe, a wether or a buck.

Price wise you are looking at around £90-£145 (around $117-$200) for a non-registered Pygmy Goat and between £145-£710 or more (Approximately $200-$1000) for a registered one, depending on lineage and the sex; for example, you could buy an unregistered wether for around £90 (around $117) whereas a registered male or female goat could set you back around £365 ($476) because you can breed them and, in the case of females, milk them.

The next expense after your goat will be fencing. Again this could cost as low as £50 ($66) if you can get the materials for free or use repurposed items or it can cost you upwards of £300 ($400) if you want an elaborate set up. It also depends on where you live and how much space you have for the enclosure. I would recommend you measure your fence and price it up before you even search for your goats because you could end up finding the fence will cost more than your actual pet.

The same goes for housing; I've known people who have built their goat sheds from sheets of corrugated iron and pallets that they've picked up for free whilst others have paid out hundreds of pounds on a brand new shed. Climate will also play a part in this cost, if you live somewhere that is hot all year round you won't need as expensive a shed because your goats will be able to live outside most of the time, whereas if you live somewhere that is often rainy and cold then your goat shed will need to be warm and free from draughts as well as fairly spacious if they are going to be spending a lot of time in it.

Your next consideration is goat toys, again you can get kids' slides and play houses or pick up wooden pallets or spools for free or you may choose to buy these. I would always use second hand items if possible for goats as it will eventually get dirty and broken. Try searching websites such as eBay or Facebook Marketplace for people in your area selling these types of items.

Next is feeding equipment and food. In the UK you can buy a hay rack for as little as £30 upwards depending on the size and quality. In the US, a hay feeder can cost you anywhere from $39.95 upwards.

The cost of their actual food will depend on how much they eat and where you buy your hay from as well as a whole host of other factors so it isn't possible for me to give an exact figure without knowing your own personal circumstances. For example, if you have storage space you may choose to buy your hay in bulk which will be cheaper. Also your goats may eat less hay if you provide more forage and vice versa therefore these costs are not exact but rather an educated estimate. In the UK you can feed two goats for around £15-£30 a month if you are feeding both hay and Pygmy Goat mix with some vegetables thrown in. In the USA costs can be as low as $20-$30 per month. You should find that your costs are lower in the summer and higher in winter as they will eat more. For example, most owners say that two goats go through around 2 bales of hay a month in the summer and double this in the winter.

Bedding costs will depend on what type you use. Straw is usually the most common as it's usually the cheapest but wood shavings or flax are other options. The price of these is dependent upon your area and the type of barn and flooring you have. If you only change it once a month and do lots of spot checks each day you can keep costs low.

The final costs to factor in are things like de-worming and vets bills. I can only really give a rough estimate because these costs are dependent on how much your vet charges, how often you take them and the reasons for going. A general yearly check-up for instance could cost you £50 per goat or a more serious problem could cost you a few hundred pounds. (Likewise in the USA it could cost you $20 to $250 depending on why you are going and how often). As these prices are per goat I would advise that you either look into getting your goats insured or put away a certain amount of money each month just in case you do need to take them to a vet for any reason.

The remaining costs are things like leashes, collars, hoof trimmers and so on which are all one off costs and can be anywhere between £50 upwards. (Or $65 upwards) for the whole lot depending on whether you buy second hand or new and whether you go for high quality or not.

All in all I believe that the costs for owning a couple of Pygmy Goats are higher in the beginning when you have to purchase your fencing and housing, et cetera but can be kept low each month when you are only purchasing food and a few supplements here and there.

I would recommend you make a list of everything you need, price it all up and start saving first then purchase your goats when you have adequate fencing and housing in place ready for them.

Chapter 2: Laws

Before you rush out and buy your adorable new pet you should consider the law in your area. Are Pygmy Goats even allowed on your property? If you're renting then it may have crossed your mind to ask permission from the landlord and if you own your house then you may nod and say "of course, I own my property and land therefore I can bring any animal I wish to live there", however it may not be this simple.

Pygmy Goats are farm animals and whatever country you live in they will be treated as livestock by the authorities even if you class your goat as a treasured family member. The phenomenon of goats as pets is still relatively new and there are numerous rules and regulations you must comply with.

UK

If you are moving into or live in a newly built area then most likely you will be prohibited from owning livestock such as goats and chickens. These are simply not allowed to be kept even as pets in these urban areas.

In the UK, if goats are allowed onto your property then you must have a holding number (CPH) for your property in order to own a goat as well as a herd number. The good news is that whilst this may sound daunting, it is simply a matter of contacting your local DEFRA (Department for Environment, Food and Rural Affairs) office and filling out a form. There isn't even any charge.

You are also required to keep a holding register for your goats which is essentially a record book which details every movement of individual animals to and from your land. You will need to record any births or deaths in this book also. It can be a paper record which is obtained from DEFRA or can be completed online using the ARAMS (Animal Reporting And Movement Service) website. Again whilst time consuming it is pretty straight forward.

When you get to the stage of finding goats to purchase you should check that the animals you want are properly identified with ear tags and/or a tattoo which shows the herd number as well as the goats' individual numbers, as goats cannot leave their birth premises unless they are identified. This is the responsibility of the breeder but because it is illegal to move a goat that is not properly earmarked it is important that you, as the buyer, check that this has been done before purchasing.

Once you have purchased your goats and are ready to move them to your land you should be handed a copy of the Animal Movement License (AML) which you should return to Trading Standards (Animal Health) within three days of moving the goat onto your land.

Each year you will also need to do an inventory of all livestock on your land even if you only have a couple of goats as pets.

If you decide that you no longer want to keep goats whether it's because they died and you don't wish to replace them or because you chose to sell them on then you will have to inform APHA (Animal and Plant Health Agency) within thirty days of the goats no longer being on your land.

Keeping medical records for Pygmy Goats is also a legal requirement and these should include vaccinations and any medicines that are administered to your individual goats.

Another law is that of the disposal of fallen stock. Not only do you have to record the death in your holding register but you need to dispose of your goat either by taking it to a pet crematorium yourself or by arranging for a licensed collector to visit your home. If you choose the latter you must keep the receipt with your records. You are not allowed to simply bury your goats on your land.

Please check the laws in your local area regarding keeping these animals as pets before you purchase them. Whilst the information contained in this book is correct at the time of going to press the legal requirements for keeping livestock changes constantly and it is advised that you contact your local DEFRA office to ensure you have the most up to date information before bringing goats onto your land.

USA

In the US you should check the zoning requirements for your town/city as some don't allow for goats or any livestock to be kept as pets. This information can be obtained from your local zoning board office or building inspector.

Be prepared to wait a while for them to come back to you with an answer because the 'keeping goat as pets' craze is still fairly new and as the municipal ordinances were drawn up many moons ago when goats were classed as farm animals not pets. They are usually only accepted in the zoning districts that are classed as agricultural and prohibited in those areas that are seen as residential.

Animals are usually regulated in several ways so you should also check the general city/town ordinances or by laws, especially any that deal with 'nuisance' animals and animal control, as sometimes goats are expressly prohibited as 'nuisance animals'.

The good news is that some cities ban large breeds of goats but allow miniature breeds as pets, so if you are looking to buy a Pygmy Goat you may be okay but again, although your city may allow goats you also need to check your homeowners association or condominium rules if these apply to you because there may be explicit rules in there.

Areas that allow miniature goats such as Pygmy or Nigerian Dwarf Goats may have specific rules regarding their care. This can include (but is not limited to) the following;

All goats must be dehorned and male goats must be neutered.

Only two goats are allowed (no more and no less).

The type of shed used to house the goats should meet specific requirements with regards to size, design and so on.

The shed must have direct access to an outdoor enclosure which should also follow strict guidelines with regards to the size (usually at least four hundred square feet), specified design, height of the fencing and so on.

Droppings must be removed and properly disposed of in a manner that prevents health issues, pests (such as flies) and water contamination.

Selling goat derived food products such as milk or meat is prohibited.

Again the above rules will vary between towns, cities and states and there may be many more that aren't mentioned here. My advice is check before you buy and don't break the law.

Whilst it can be frustrating to be told you can't have the pet you desire or to be waiting weeks or even months for answer, remember that it can be just as confusing for the authorities to interpret the antiquated rules when it comes to keeping goats as pets.

If you do initially get turned down, don't be discouraged. It is possible in some circumstances to get the rules changed, for example, a girl that suffered with anxiety was allowed to keep a pygmy goat by stating it was a doctor recommended companion animal. Whilst I'm not suggesting you run to the doctors just because you have been told you can't have a pet goat the example does highlight the fact that rules can be changed and as the rules were made before goats became pets. It may be worth writing to your local council member to see if they can look at the laws and help you get permission to keep a couple of miniature goats, showing evidence that they are now be classed as 'back yard' pets.

Neighbours

You might not ordinarily care what your neighbours think about what you do but you should, out of courtesy, consider how your neighbours feel about you keeping goats in your back garden.

Some Pygmy Goats can be loud and whilst they are usually only really vocal around dinner time or when they're in heat, the noise may still annoy your neighbours.

Secondly, goats smell. They are farm animals after all and your neighbours may not appreciate the odour that emanates from your yard once your new pets arrive, especially when the weather is warm.

Thirdly, piles of manure not only look unpleasant but an untidy enclosure can attract flies and other pests which again, can become a nuisance to your neighbours should they wish to sit out in their back yard.

Goats are also great escape artists and your neighbours may not be very happy to find that your goat has gotten out and eaten their prize roses or taken the washing off their line.

Any of the above could lead to friction between you and those who live around you and could result in them reporting you to the authorities or in some extreme cases could lead to them taking matters into their own hands.

I would suggest you have a conversation with all your neighbours before you purchase your goats and if they have any reservations reassure them that smells, noise, and so on will all be dealt with immediately before the goats become a nuisance to them. If you have a good relationship with your neighbours then they probably won't mind as long as they know that you will clean up the mess and it won't affect them. If they don't then whilst it is entirely up to you (assuming the authorities are allowing it) I would think carefully about whether it is worth alienating your neighbours just because you want a couple of goats.

Chapter 3: Before Buying

Research
This is something I would always recommend to anyone regardless of what pet they are buying but I believe it is especially important for creatures like these that are not traditional pets like cats and dogs.

Reading books such as this one and visiting websites is a good start.

Secondly, I would recommend that you join forums and social media groups that are dedicated to Pygmy Goats and ask questions to find out the ins and outs of buying and caring for these animals. If you haven't found a breeder then you could also ask for recommendations. I think that even if you have found a breeder you are happy with it is worth asking whether anyone has heard of them as someone else may have used them previously and can tell you both good and bad things about them.

Connecting with other goat owners before you buy is great because you are building up a network which you could then use should you buy a goat and need help or advice in the future. Usually owners are happy to talk to new owners and share their experience and knowledge.

I would also advise that you speak to a vet that specialises in Pygmy Goats and ask them for advice on what to look for when you purchase. They may also have a price list so that you can get an idea of the cost of both buying these creatures and also vet bills in your area. This is a good way to ensure you are not being ripped off with your initial purchase and can also give you an indication of whether you can afford to keep these animals in the long term or not.

Registered Or Unregistered?
It is always better to purchase a registered goat if possible because they have lineage that can be tracked, similar to a 'pedigree' dog.

Although it doesn't really matter that your goats aren't registered, if you are just keeping a couple as pets it is worth remembering that if you buy a registered goat you will be able to enter them into shows.

From a breeding or selling point of view, registered goats are easier to sell because you can show the background records to potential buyers. If you have it in your mind that you may breed your goats in future then always buy registered animals, as if you breed goats that aren't registered their kids cannot be registered. These days more and more people are looking to purchase registered Pygmy Goats so I would never recommend breeding non-registered ones.

Whilst you are probably only just looking into purchasing goats you should think about what might happen in the future should your circumstances change; you may not think you will ever need to but should you have to re-home your goats in the future it will be a lot easier to do so if they are both registered as their new owners may want to breed or show them.

A registered goat costs more which is a disadvantage for someone looking for a pet, however it also means that if you do breed or sell your goats they will be worth more.

The flipside of course is that if you are just looking for a couple of pets then do you really need a registered goat? You may want to save the money and not bother if you have no intention to breed or show them.

Questions To Ask A Breeder

It is important that you know what to look for when purchasing a Pygmy Goat so that you can be certain that you are buying a healthy animal.

Write down a list of questions that you want to ask the breeders before you decide whether to purchase or not. These should include (but are not limited to) the following:

Have the goats all been tested for CL, CAE and Johnes? If the answer to this question is no then leave immediately! Most likely the answer will be yes in which case you should ask the breeder to provide you with the results. Never take a seller's word no matter how friendly and trustworthy they appear to be. A genuine seller will care about their animals and will be happy to provide any evidence to prove that they are healthy.

What goat organization is the breeder registered with? There are many to choose from and there isn't really one that is better than the other but all breeders should be associated with a goat organization so that you can be reassured that their goats are registered. In the UK these include the Pygmy Goat Club UK and the British Goat Society. In America there is the National Pygmy Goat Association (NPGA) amongst others.

Can I have photographs? This only really applies if you are searching online and enquiring via email rather than viewing the goats in person. Whilst I would always recommend visiting the goats before you buy them it is a good idea to ask for pictures before travelling a long way. Don't settle for just one picture but decide which goats you are interested in then ask the breeder to send you photographs of these goats from different angles so that you are able to see that they are healthy and in good condition.

Can I See The Paperwork? If you are buying a registered goat it is advised that you ask the breeder to have all the paperwork ready so that it can be passed over at the time of the sale. If you are not collecting your goats in person then ask them to email you a copy (or send a photograph of the paperwork) so that you are certain it is all ready and waiting. There are lots of stories on the Internet of people who have been fobbed off by breeders promising to send paperwork only to discover months (or even years) down the line that the paperwork never existed and the goat has never been registered yet they have paid the higher price thinking that they were.

You may also want to ask about the appraisal and production records, as these will tell you how several of the goat's characteristics stack up in comparison to other's in their herd which may be important if you do want to breed or show these animals.

What is the personality and pedigree of the goats like? As mentioned previously, a registered goat should mean you can trace their lineage and the breeder should be able to provide details of their pedigree.

It is important that you ask about the goats' personalities so that you can find one that is suited to you and your home. For instance, if you want a family pet then you should tell the breeder this and they should have an idea of which of their goats will be suited to children and which ones might not.

Visiting the goats will allow you to see if you are compatible together. Although Pygmy Goats generally are friendly, their personalities can vary and some goats are stand offish whilst others are downright unfriendly. If you can meet the goat first you will get an idea of whether you like it or not. Also, goats will like certain people and not others so you may have a goat that is described as 'standoffish' yet when you meet it may take a liking to you and you may discover that it is more affectionate than you thought. Likewise, the same is also true; one that has affectionate parents may take an instant disliking to humans and not want to bond with you.
Once you meet a goat in person you can decide whether or not you have time to work with them or whether they are too temperamental and you won't be able to train them.

Another reason to visit in person if you've never had goats before is that once you've visited a breeder you may decide that they are too noisy or too smelly and are not suitable for the area in which you live. It is better to discover this before you purchase than afterwards.

What food have the goats been eating? It is important to know what food the goats have been raised on. Some breeders will give you an extensive list and specific brands and may even provide you with a couple of weeks' worth of food but if they don't you should make sure you are clear about what the goats have been eating and if possible, where you can purchase either the same food or similar. This is because a dramatic change in their diet can lead to stomach upsets which can mean you end up with a very sick goat and possibly high vet bills before your new pet has even settled in properly.

Horns

Okay this isn't really a question but you should be aware that whilst Pygmy Goats look lovely with horns these can be dangerous for you as an owner and your family, as well as other pets and even to the goat itself. You may decide you like horns but just be aware that a goat with horns charging at full pelt can cause A LOT of damage. As tiny as these goats are, personally I wouldn't risk it with children or other animals. Before buying you may want to ask the breeder if their goats are polled – which means naturally hornless – or whether they have their goats disbudded – which means removing the buds on the babies before they can grow into horns. (See Chapter 9)

What has the worming procedure and general maintenance been? Again, to keep the care consistent and make the transition between the place they were born and your home as easy as possible for your new pets it is important you know how the goats have been raised. Ask any questions you can think of relating to the general maintenance of your new goats.

Have any of your goats died for unexplained reasons? This may be an uncomfortable question to ask but it is an important one because if the answer is yes then it may not be wise to buy from that breeder. Of course not all breeders will tell the truth but if you are asking in person you may be able to tell if they are lying or not.

Can I contact other buyers for references or speak with the herds' vet? Some breeders may say no and I'm not suggesting that those who do are bad sellers that are selling dodgy animals; some may refuse purely because they have a confidentiality policy and don't like passing on clients' details and this is perfectly fine. However, very good breeders should have some testimonials on their website or social media pages and you may be able to contact previous buyers this way. If not, the breeder should at least be willing to give you their vet's contact details so that you can, if you wish to do so, contact them and ask about the health of the goats.

Extras

You may just want a Pygmy Goat to keep as a pet and not really care what it looks like as long as it's healthy. This is the stance I would take as I believe that animals that are bred to have certain traits can also end up having medical problems. However, some people do look for ones that have unusual traits such as blue eyes, moon spots or particular colours. If you have seen a goat that appeals to you because of its unusual characteristics then this may be something you want to enquire about when approaching breeders.

Remember – DON'T BE AFRAID TO SAY NO!

You may travel for miles to see a goat that you are interested in purchasing but if you are unsure then don't feel pressurized into buying. You may be desperate for a pet goat (well two!) but always walk away if you hear the metaphorical alarm bells ringing. There are plenty more sellers even if you have to wait a while longer or spend a bit more money. If it means you are getting a healthier animal that is better suited to you and your home then it is worth it.

As it can be disappointing to travel a long way only to find that the goats aren't what you were expecting I would recommend you email a few breeders first, listing your questions and asking for photographs and proof of health testing and registration so that you can be reassured that the breeder(s) you do visit are more than likely going to have suitable, healthy goats. From their replies you may also build up a rapport and find one that you think is more trustworthy just from the way they converse with you and how helpful they are.

Red Flags
Whilst it may be difficult to know if someone is telling the truth or not, if you come across any of the following from a seller you should go elsewhere:

Lack of medical records, especially the results of tests for CAE, CL and Johnes.

A reluctance to send pictures or only sending one or two from the same angle.

Lack of paperwork or unwillingness to send it; someone giving lots of excuses as to why it isn't ready could be an indicator that the paperwork doesn't exist.

Lack of information about the goats' parentage.

Poor living conditions; too many goats and not enough land is usually an indicator of a bad seller and if the goats are living in unsuitable conditions from birth, chances are they will have health problems.

Unhealthy looking goats - this is another reason why it is important to see a goat before purchasing it. If you can see the other goats in the herd it was born into you can see for yourself whether they look healthy or not. Don't buy a goat because you feel sorry for it, again, if it looks unhealthy it probably is.

Signs Of A Healthy Goat

Whilst it can be difficult to determine whether an animal is healthy unless you are a qualified vet, there are some signs you can look for to reduce the chances of buying a sick goat.

You should try to assess the following:

Eyes – these should be bright and not dull or sick looking.

Hooves – these should be properly trimmed as overgrown feet can cause leg problems in the future as well as conditions such as Foot Rot. (See Chapter 7 – Common Illnesses)

Coat – this should be smooth and glossy with no lumps or cuts.

Skin – this should be pliable and clean. There should be no lumps or bumps as these could signal abscesses which are highly contagious.

Body – You should be able to feel the goats' ribs under their skin but their bones shouldn't jut out.

Tail – this should be upright or relaxed, not tucked in.

Knees – should be smooth not knobbly, as knobbly knees can often be an indicator of CAE.

Stance – the goats should look relaxed and not be hunched up.

Faeces/manure – not the nicest thing to study but you should check when you visit a herd that any droppings you see are firm, slightly moist pellets or balls rather than clumpy piles or runny messes. Check colouring too as very dark faeces may be this colour because they contain blood. You could look online beforehand to get an idea of what healthy faeces for these animals look like.

Urine – you may not see the goat urinate but if you do you should take note of whether it does so easily and without any effort or signs of pain.

Personality – as mentioned previously, goats are all different but generally if you are looking for a pet, choose one that is friendly rather than extremely shy or aggressive.

There may be other things that have not been mentioned above and it may be worth looking at photographs of healthy and unhealthy goats to give you an idea of what to look for when searching for one to buy.

Other Considerations
There may be other considerations aside from health and appearance to factor in depending on why you are buying a goat.

Family Pet
As you are reading this book you clearly want a Pygmy Goat as a pet, therefore you should choose a doe or wether that is free of any major defects or health problems and whether they have a steep rump or incorrect breed character shouldn't matter to you. Really you just want to make sure that they have a friendly personality and will suit you and your family.

With this in mind I would try to choose a goat that was bottle fed as a kid, as these tend to be friendlier towards humans than those that were raised by their mothers. Secondly I would get one without horns, as mentioned above these are just too dangerous to have as a family pet so look for either a naturally polled goat or one that has been disbudded at a young age.

Milk Provider
If you also want a pet that provides milk then you will be looking for something slightly different. For instance, clearly you want a female that is either pregnant or just had a baby unless you are intending to breed her yourself – despite what some people believe only females provide milk and only when they have been bred. Secondly, you will want one that is friendly, gentle, easy to milk and co-operative, especially if you have no experience. Thirdly, you will need to check that she has the correct sized teats and good strong udder attachment as a saggy, baggy udder can easily be damaged and can also be too low to get a bucket under.

For goats that will be milked you should check that the female hasn't any defects that will make birthing complicated. Whilst she doesn't have to be show quality, some faults could hinder kidding and/or milk production, for instance, bad feet or weak posture could lead to difficulties with walking and eating in the future. To continually get milk from your female you will need to continue to breed her each year.

Lastly you should check that your goat comes from a family that has a history of providing good quality milk in fairly high quantities.

Show Pet
You may decide that you don't want a pet that you can milk but that you do want one to enter in shows or breed. If this is the case then you need to not only check for good general health but you will also need to purchase a registered goat that comes complete with papers.

A show standard goat also needs to be conformationally correct and as close to 'ideal' as possible. This means no faults such as winged shoulders, bad feet, weak posture, steep rumps and so on.

Where To Buy
There are a variety of places where you can purchase a Pygmy Goat and whilst I won't recommend one over the other – just like there are good and bad pet stores there are good and bad auctions, good and bad breeders and good and bad owners – I will try to list both the advantages and disadvantages of each. Often where you buy depends on the area in which you live, for instance, the only place reachable

to you may be an auction or you may only have breeders available in your area.

As mentioned before, do your research; just because you know of one breeder in your area don't settle for them but look for others too, even if they are further afield, just in case you decide the nearest breeders' goats aren't of a high standard.

Auction
It may seem the most obvious and therefore the best place to purchase a goat from. This is because when most people think of goats they associate them with farms and therefore with animal auctions.

However, auctions are not always advisable because you won't be able to find out the history of the animals and those bought at auctions may already have illnesses or other problems that you won't know about until after you've purchased. This can be expensive if you end up paying for unexpected vet bills but if you have other animals on your land already it can be catastrophic.

If you are going to purchase from an auction I would recommend that you ask about to see if you can find anyone who purchased from there in the past and find out what their experiences were like.

Local Shows
This is a good starting point to search for a goat, especially if you have the intention to breed. You can quickly build up a herd just by owning a couple of female goats and hiring a stud for mating.

Local goat shows are good because you will be able to study the goats that are considered 'good' specimens and listen to the judges' explanations as to why one placed higher than the other. Whilst this may not interest you (unless you want to enter your new pet into shows) visiting local shows are a great way to meet both owners and breeders and make contact with the local goat community. Many will be happy to discuss their animals, provide advice and tell stories about the joys of owning a goat as well as recommending breeders if they don't have any for sale themselves.

You never know, you may come across a reputable breeder that has goats already for sale and if you get to know them beforehand they may even do you a deal.

Local Breeders

It is always a good idea to find and visit a few breeders so you can compare the animals and their living conditions as well as the breeders themselves.

Of course you may not have a lot nearby in which case I would suggest speaking to several via email and telephone before you choose which one to visit. Ask the questions mentioned earlier and any others you may have. A responsible breeder will be only too happy to provide photographs and information about the kids that are for sale and their parents even if you haven't decided to purchase from them yet.

Make sure you explain exactly what you are looking for in a goat and explain the living arrangements you will have for your potential new pets, for instance the amount of land space available, the type of fencing you have in place as well as how you intend to house your goats, whether you have other animals on your property and if so what kind, as well as mentioning if you have children or not. This will all help the breeder to match up the goats with you and your lifestyle so you can be confident they will have a suitable one available when you visit.

If they provide you with advice then take this on board as it is a sign that they are concerned about their goats and who they sell them to. For instance a breeder may tell you that you don't have enough space or suggest that you build your barn first or do more research before purchasing. I doubt very much that one would refuse to sell you a goat – unless you are adamant you are only going to keep one rather than a pair or they're really concerned about the goats' welfare with you but if they do I would listen to their reasons why rather than getting angry and blaming them as a breeder.

Chapter 4: Feeding

If you look on the Internet for information about feeding Pygmy Goats you will find that there is very little available and what there is can be scattered about over hundreds of different pages. When you do find anything it is often conflicting information which can be quite confusing.

Don't let this lack of information put you off, feeding goats is fairly simple; they are herbivores and therefore eat plant based foods.

How Does A Goat's Stomach Work?
Feeding a goat is easier if you understand how their digestion system works.

Goats are classified as ruminants, meaning that instead of having one compartment in their stomach like we humans do, they have four. As the plant material is eaten it travels through each chamber in turn and the nutrients are extracted.

The first three compartments contain tiny microorganisms which break down the food that the goat eats. These microbes are actually living creatures and as such need to be kept healthy in order to keep your goat healthy. These microbes can be upset if the goat's diet is changed suddenly, which is why you should always introduce new foods slowly.

If you have ever watched a goat eat you may notice that sometimes they appear to inhale their food rather than chew it slowly. This rapidly consumed food is stored in the first and largest of the four chambers known as the rumen. This food will later be regurgitated and chewed at a more leisurely pace known as 'chewing the cud' or 'ruminating'.

As disgusting as this may sound to us it is important your goat does this as it assists the micro-organisms to break down the fibrous material and extract the nutrients. Once food reaches the final chamber – the abomasum – it is then processed in the same way as it would be in a single stomached animal.

What To Feed
Hay
Goats are designed to process fibrous plant material and therefore hay and plants should comprise the main bulk of their diet.

There are two main types of hay; leguminous hay such as alfalfa and clover and non-leguminous hay made from green crops like barley and oats.

The former have higher protein levels and will contain more calcium. Non-leguminous hay is often thought to be inferior and less palatable, however it can be rich in carbohydrates. A good compromise therefore is a mix of high quality leguminous and grass hay.

How much they eat depends on age, sex and condition, for example, a pregnant female will eat more than an adult wether,

Only use high quality hay that has been stored correctly. Mouldy hay can not only make your goat sick but is also a fire hazard.

Hay should be available all the time, even for those goats that forage all day.

Goats are notorious for picking out the tastiest pieces of food and throwing the rest away so it is often more economical to use feeders which are designed to prevent this waste. These feeders usually have bars spaced 4-5 inches apart which allows the goat to reach the hay but prevents them from sticking their head in to pull it all out.

Another popular option are hay bags, however many people don't like these because there are many horror stories circulating about goats becoming entangled and strangling themselves. If you do prefer to use one then my advice would be to only do so if you are around to constantly supervise your goat when they're using it.

Foraging

It is a myth that goats will eat tin cans and trampolines and anything else they happen to come across so don't worry too much if you leave a lawn chair or two out. It is also a misconception that goats will eat the whole of your lawn so that you will no longer have to mow it. They are browsers rather than grazers and whilst they may indeed eat patches of your lawn they will not eat the whole thing all in one go. They tend to be opportunistic feeders meaning that if they happen to stumble along your prized pansies during a foraging session they will most likely snap them up rather than eat your lawn so keep this in mind when you are allowing them free roam of your garden. However, they are not picky so whether it is a freshly grown sapling they find or a pile of weeds they will eat it.

It is important to allow access to natural outside vegetation that they can forage themselves as this provides them with exercise and also reduces the amount of hay you need to feed them. The advantage of keeping these animals as pets is that plants we consider weeds will make a tasty meal for them so whilst you may still need to mow your lawn once in a while, you shouldn't have to pull up too many weeds anymore!

To prevent damaging their rumens or developing an overeating disease known as Enterotoxaemia, different vegetation should be introduced slowly to your goat every spring.

Toxic Plants

Before letting your goat(s) roam free and eat whatever they like you should be aware of what plants are growing in their outdoor enclosure as some plants can be extremely poisonous to goats.

Plants such as Azaleas, Laburnum, Hemlock, Rhubarb, Laurel, yew, honeysuckle, alder, Rhododendrons and evergreen shrubs are all extremely toxic, as are the green stuff from flowers such as delphiniums or bulbous plants such as tulips and daffodils and these should all be removed from any area that the goat is going to be let loose in. Make sure you do a thorough check of your garden, preferably before your goat comes to live with you.

There is a long list of plants that are toxic to goats available on the Internet and there's far too many for me to list in this book. Not only that but the list is constantly changing as people post that a certain plant isn't toxic whilst a new one may appear on the list so for the most up to date information it is better to do a quick Google search.

Not only is it impractical for me to list them all here, it is also impossible to remove them all from any garden, especially if you have a lot of land. The guidance therefore is to find the ones that are the most toxic and remove those and make sure there is plenty of other vegetation for them to choose from. Usually if a goat has access to plenty of non-toxic plants they will usually avoid (or at least just have a nibble) on those that are mildly toxic to them which means they shouldn't get ill.

What If There Aren't Many Plants To Forage?
If you don't have access to a pasture and your goat is being kept in a small enclosure that doesn't have many plants available or your goat eats them too quickly for them to grow back, you can go out and forage plants for them yourself and scatter them about in your back garden. Plants that are good include dandelion, nettles, kale, thistle, multiflora rose and chicory. They also like sweetcorn husks and stalks, carrots, kale, turnips, pumpkins and beets. Just ensure that the plants you give them are free from pesticides and other potentially harmful chemicals, if you are foraging from surrounding land you may want to give food a good wash first before feeding.

Another idea, depending on how much land you have available, would be to section off part of your garden away from your goats where you can grow plants for their food. This way they can't get to them before they're fully grown and you can be absolutely certain that they are safe for your goat and free from chemicals.

Minerals
Goats need vitamins and minerals to keep healthy. Some of this they will receive from their hay but this alone isn't enough to supply them with all the vitamins and minerals they need. Even the amount found in hay can vary depending on where it is grown, therefore it is recommended to feed them a separate mineral to prevent vitamin and mineral deficiencies.

When buying goat mineral look for one that includes both calcium and phosphorous, as these two minerals are necessary to build healthy, strong bones and helps females make milk.

The ratio is very important and should be 2:1, which means two parts calcium to one part phosphorous. Often ten percent calcium to eight percent phosphorous is a common way to see it listed.

Mineral mix should also contain salt and Vitamins A, D and E are often added as is Ammonium Chloride, which helps prevent urinary calculi which is common in male goats. Most will also have small amounts of copper, zinc, magnesium, potassium, manganese and selenium.

Water

All living creatures need access to fresh water in order to thrive and Pygmy Goats are no different. In fact they need plenty of water in order to keep their rumens in good working order. For males, water can help prevent urinary calculi and keep their urinary tracts healthy and as goat's milk is mainly comprised of water it is especially important if you have lactating does.

Some goats can be very particular and some owners report that their goat will refuse to drink because there is a bit of dirt in the water or because it didn't taste right to them, so ensure it is always clean and fresh and change it periodically throughout the day.

If you find your goat doesn't seem to be drinking much water, especially in the winter months, try giving them warm water as they seem to enjoy this more than icy cold water, so warming their water slightly can increase their intake.

In the summer months you may find they are drinking more because of the sunshine. If you have extremely hot weather it may be a good idea to put ice mixed with water in buckets around the goats' enclosure or in their water trough. This will eventually melt, ensuring your goats always have access to fresh water. This is particularly important if you are out during the day for long periods.

Any does that you are milking or who are nursing will need to replenish the water they have lost in providing milk so always make sure there is plenty of water available after you have finished milking and throughout the day.

Clean water is the cheapest, yet most important nutrient in your goats' diet so make sure that there is always a generous supply available and it is easily accessible to them.

Grain
If you are giving grain then this should only comprise around ten percent of a Pygmy Goat's diet. However, it is worth noting that there are mixed opinions with regards to grain. Some owners say that their goats become moody and describe them as "spoilt brats" when they get grain whilst others say that a small amount is fine. Goats don't need grain to survive and they will live happily on pasture, hay or a combination of both but for pregnant or lactating does, growing kids and bucks in rut it can be a good, quick source of energy. It is also believed that grain can help keep their body heat up when it's cold at night so if you are in an area that is incredibly cold you may want to consider feeding grain in the winter.

It is thought that feeding grain can improve milk quality, so it is a good way to provide extra vitamins, minerals and proteins for pregnant or lactating does.

However, grain can cause weight gain, bloating and digestive upsets if too much is eaten so only feed in moderation and don't overdo it. For pregnant does half a cup of grain will suffice and can be increased to one cup a hundred days into their pregnancy and when they're being milked.

For kids and rutting or breeding males then a quarter to half a cup of grain per day should be enough.

Adult males who aren't being bred and wethers shouldn't be given grain as it can increase the chances of urinary calculi.

Scraps And Treats

A question many people ask me is 'do you feed your goat leftover scraps from your kitchen?' The answer is yes. There's no reason why you can't do this as long as you remember that goats are herbivores and therefore only eat plant based foods so don't go giving them a Sunday roast covered in gravy!

Fruit and vegetables are perfectly fine and you will find that your Pygmy Goat will love orange, apples and bananas – peel and all.

Many people worry that different foods will change the flavour of their goats' milk and I'm sure that if you fed certain things in high quantities such as forty or fifty garlic cloves then it would be enough to affect the milk flavour, however scraps here and there in small amounts shouldn't affect it at all.

Other treats include carrots, raisins, sunflower seeds, pumpkin and pumpkin seeds and greens.

Remember these scraps and treats should only be fed in moderation and, as mentioned above, introduced individually and very slowly into their diet so as not to upset your goats' stomachs.

Store Bought Goat Feed

Stores will try to promote goat feed and new owners will often buy it thinking it is something their Pygmy Goat needs. Unfortunately, what they don't realise is that most of these feeds are comprised of grain. The owners unwittingly feed their goats this and because they can't really handle more than ten percent of grain in their diet they quickly become ill. This is because a high amount of grain produces acidosis, which is an imbalance of acid in their bodies. As goats are meant to be more alkaline than acid they get very sick and experience pain, bloating, constipation, skin problems and it can lead to death.

If you do purchase goat feed then read the bag carefully and only give it in very small amounts alongside hay and foraged foods.

Supplements

Other than the minerals mentioned above, goats don't really need any added supplements. You can sometimes boost a goat's health occasionally if necessary so it is sometimes helpful to keep a stock of the following:

Black Oil Sunflower Seeds – These make a great treat for your goat and can be bought from pet stores or anywhere else that sells goat feed. They will give your goat a shiny coat and healthy skin. For lactating goats you can add a little into their grain mixture after milking.

Probiotics – This helps poor rumen function however you shouldn't give it to your goats all the time as it's just not necessary. If your goat is getting over a major illness or is coming to the end of a course of antibiotics then probiotics may help them, however always make sure you use one specifically for ruminant animals otherwise you could end up doing more harm than good.

Baking Soda – You can pick this up from your local supermarket and it is great for stomach upsets or bloating as it can help rebalance the PH in their rumens. If you do suspect bloating or digestive problems it is always wise to consult a vet first before administering this supplement.

Herbal De-wormer Mix – This should be given every six months in order to de-worm your goats and keep them healthy.

Points To Remember

Goats can easily become bored of your lawn and move onto weeds, rose bushes and trees – both the bark and the leaves – so make sure they have a good variety of foods. If you have particular plants you are precious about and don't want your goats to eat then ensure these are far away from your goats' enclosure.

A nutritious diet equals healthier goats. Although you are probably only thinking of buying a couple of goats to keep as pets you may eventually decide that you would like to breed your animals or have them provide milk so it is worth noting here that there have been studies that have shown a direct correlation between a high quality diet and increased fertility and healthier kids as well as an increase in birth weight.

Remember to keep your goats diet simple; a variety of green plants; foraged, hay and pasture – with the odd vegetable treat now and then is enough to keep your goats happy. Keep grains to a minimum and avoid tin cans and other junk and you and your goat should be happy.

Always check the calcium and phosphorous levels in any grain, store bought feed, minerals and supplements you are giving to ensure they are balanced in your goats' diet, too much or too little of either or both can lead to your goat becoming ill.

Chapter 5: Fencing And Housing

If you ask somebody who owns goats how you can tell if your fence is good enough to keep your goats safe you may get the reply "throw a bucket of water at it; if the water can get through then so can your goats." This is a popular saying which highlights the fact that goats can pretty much get out of anything if they have a mind to do so.

One mistake many first time goat owners make is they assume that a fence is a fence and as long as there are no holes in it then their existing one should be fine. They may look docile and cute but they are incredibly witty so don't underestimate them.

You may be lucky and end up with a couple that aren't interested in escaping but most goats will try to jump over, crawl under, climb or stand on, lean against or squeeze through pretty much any boundary they come across so I would strongly recommend that you invest in a good fence from the very beginning to save time and money having to replace it later.

There are so many different options for goat fencing that it can be daunting. You need your fence to keep your goats enclosed but also to keep any predators out. It needs to be strong enough that it can't be knocked over easily or blown down by high winds. It also needs to be high enough that your goats can't jump or climb over it.

It may sound simple enough but these goats are very cunning escape artists and it is amazing to see them squeeze under a fence that you thought was impenetrable.

Many people will use cattle fencing but this can be quite flimsy so I would avoid this.

Another option is chain link and whilst it is possible to climb, Pygmy Goats may find it difficult. What they do tend to do however is push on the bottom of any fence to get to the grass on the other side. The problem with chain link is that as soon as it gives a little the goats will push harder so unless the fence has been anchored at the bottom to something incredibly strong that won't give under pressure eventually, the links will separate. I'm not saying it will happen immediately but over time your goats may manage to get through a chain link fence. They will then devour anything tasty on the other side which, if you're keeping as pets and not living on a large farm, will be your neighbours' garden. They're also at risk of being hurt by dogs and other predators so it really is in your best interest to keep your goats as safe as possible.

A third option is welded wire fencing which are squares welded together. These squares will come in many different sizes and it tends to be one of the cheapest options but many owners will say to avoid this because the goats will stand on and rub themselves along the fencing which eventually causes the welds to break.

So what are your options for fencing?

You're really left with woven wire fencing or electric fencing.

Woven wire fencing is squares woven at the corners. Whilst these fences tend to be sturdy they also tend to be the most expensive BUT as it will withstand more wear and tear it is often better to pay more upfront rather than having to constantly repair or replace it.

This type of fencing comes in different size squares; usually 2x4 inches, 4x4 inches and 6x6 inches. The smaller the square the more costly the fence, which means you could be tempted to use 6x6 inches just to keep the cost down. However, for miniature breeds like Pygmy Goats it is recommended that you use 2x4 inches otherwise they may stick their heads through and risk getting stuck in the larger squares which can not only cause injury to them but can make them vulnerable to predators until you are able to come to their rescue. Babies can also squeeze through the holes and escape.

Your final option is electric fencing which uses high tensile wire connected to a charger to electrify it. Up to seven strands is usually enough to suffice.

These are fairly easy to install and can be fairly cheap in comparison to the woven wire fencing. If you train your goats to stay away from it, make sure your fence is always charged properly and the bottom wire is kept away from grass or other plants.

Whilst they can work by themselves the ideal would be a combination of woven wire fencing with electric strands at the top and the bottom. The electric strands at the bottom should be on the outside of the fence as this will help keep predators out whilst the strands at the top will keep your goats from jumping or climbing over it.

Goat fencing is confusing because there are a lot of options and there are a lot of ideas about what works and what doesn't. A lot of advice is also for larger breeds of goats too so make sure that if you are searching on the internet for ideas you are getting information related specifically for Pygmy Goats.

What works for one goat owner may not necessarily be suitable for another and it is dependent on how determined and curious your goats are.

I am recommending a combination of woven wire and electric because this is what works best for the majority of goat owners but you should also take into account the size and layout of your land. Electric fencing may not be suitable if you have other peoples' property connected to yours so always take this into consideration as well.

Once you've decided on the type of fence, you will be wondering how tall you need it. Most people recommend a minimum of 4 feet high for these little goats, I personally always prefer to go taller if possible.

Fence Posts

It can be very tempting to cut corners when you are building a fence, especially when you know you are getting a miniature goat that looks so sweet and innocent. Don't be fooled, Pygmy Goats are stronger than they appear and my advice is to follow the guidelines for fencing standard livestock when you are installing fence posts.

Make sure that your posts are sturdy and fixed correctly. A general rule of thumb is that when you are erecting a fence then one third of the height of the post should be fixed into the ground so for a post that is around 7-8 feet, 2-2.5 feet of fence post should be in the ground. It is worth marking your posts BEFORE setting them in so that you don't put them in too deep and make your fence too short or not put them in deep enough and risk making your fence less sturdy.

Remember you will also need a few inches extra at the top so if you are installing a six foot fence you will want six foot and a few inches of fence post sticking out of the ground in order to have enough room to securely attach the top of your fence.

The most tension will be on the corners and near the gate so this is where you will want to install H-braces. You could also add diagonal wire bracing as well at these points so that it puts opposite tension on the fence so the wire should be attached at the bottom of the corner post and run to the top of the H-brace attached to the next fence post.

Try to keep fence posts no more than ten feet apart for the main fence run and no more than eight feet apart where your H-braces are located as this will provide extra support. Whilst this rule generally works best it does depend on the type of fence you use and the size of it so do research and ask the people you are buying it from for their input too before installing.

One thing people do forget about is the soil that they are digging into. You may find that your posts are secure simply by digging a hole, putting the fence post in and shovelling the soil back around it but if you live in an area where the soil is soft or even sandy then this may not be enough and you may find that your posts start to wiggle and lean after a while. Pound your fence posts in as hard as you can and secure the posts with concrete if possible. Whilst this makes it more time consuming and expensive it is better to have a secure fence then one that is going to fall over at the slightest touch (or head butt!).

Housing

Goats aren't that particular with their shelter but when building one you should consider the following;

Can you enter and exit the shelter easily? Remember you will need to do a routine clean and therefore it needs to be accessible for you as well as your goats.

Will there be running water and electricity nearby? This will make it a whole lot easier when you are cleaning, feeding and watering your goats. There should be electric lights inside that are out of reach of your goats.

Do you have room to put a store nearby for your goat feed, bedding, toys and other supplies? Again this just makes the care a lot easier. If you are alternating toys then you will need a shed big enough to keep these in when they're not in use.

Is it well ventilated without being draughty? A stable door is useful as you can open the top part to let in some air whilst keeping the bottom closed if you don't want to let your goats out for whatever reason.

Can you insulate your enclosure? If you live in a warm climate then your goats may not have an issue with this but if you live somewhere that gets very, very cold then you may need to consider insulating your shed or using heat pads. Pygmy Goats are good at adjusting to temperatures but your shelter needs to prevent draughts and keep them dry in wet conditions as they can be susceptible to Pneumonia.

Is there enough room to provide toys? Goats are very active and in wet weather they may be inside a lot but they still need to keep themselves occupied so you should try and put in a small climbing or play area such as little platforms made of pallets or crates.

Are there glass windows? If you are buying a ready built shed then the answer to this may be yes but you need to replace these with Perspex or protect them with mesh to avoid any accidental breakages.

Can you separate your goats if you need to? If you buy your goats from the same owner then they ought to get along but if you bring two goats from two different places together then you may need to separate them, at least in the beginning. Other reasons you may need to separate your goats in the future is if one becomes ill or if you are planning to breed. They can be separated easily by hurdles or you could build stalls in your shelter. How you are going to separate needs to be considered when you are planning your shed as it will be more difficult further down the line.

No matter how lovely your goat shed is don't think that your goats will be happy to sit in their own stall day in and day out. Access from the shed should lead into a well fenced area to allow them to breathe fresh air, exercise and play together. Goats are sociable and need companionship so should be allowed to roam about their enclosures, both inside and out, together.

Size
The size of your barn or shelter depends on how big you are planning your herd to be and of course how much land you have available. For Pygmy Goats an 8 by 10 foot sturdy garden shed should be sufficient for two or three goats. It can possibly be smaller if you live in a hot country where your goats will spend the majority of their time outside but consider both winter and summer and whether they are likely to be in or out more in each season. If you live somewhere that is wet and cold and your goats are going to be

inside a lot during winter months then you will need a lot of toys and climbing areas for them.

One mistake people make is they buy two goats, build a shed big enough but then decide to breed not thinking about the fact that they will need more space once the babies are born. If you think that you may buy more goats in the future or you may want to breed one of your pets then build it bigger at the very beginning.

Of course it all depends on the amount of space you have to begin with. If you have enough space available then I would always recommend you build bigger anyway. If you don't add to your herd then you have a large shelter for your goats – it's not a bad thing and they will be very happy with the extra space.

A goat shelter doesn't have to be super expensive; if you are good with your hands (or know someone who is) then you can build it yourself out of new or recycled materials. As long as it is sturdy and practical with enough space and free from draughts it really doesn't matter what it's made from.

Flooring
This isn't something people often think about when they are considering purchasing goats but it is important and you should consider the advantages and disadvantages of each option and decide which is better suited for you and your animals.

Wooden floors can be warm and dry but they can also absorb urine and have a tendency to rot.

Concrete is great because urine can't run off and you can simply wash it down with a hose. However, it does require frequent cleaning and as it can be cold in winter you will need thick bedding.

Earthen floor is your last option and is probably the easiest type with goats as it is easy to maintain because excess urine drains away and it requires a lot less cleaning and bedding changes. As soil is warmer and more comfortable for goats than wood or concrete you don't need to use as much bedding. Whilst you will need to do the occasional deep clean to keep bacteria levels and insects at bay, if you do daily spot checks these deep cleans can just be done once or twice a year if you have a soil floor.

Shade

You will need to provide your goat with shade to allow them to get out of the sun as well as an indoor shelter. This can be as simple as putting a table under a large tree or adding a platform with a ramp to the side of your barn so your goat can sit underneath for shade or climb on top to sit in the sun or play. If you do add some sort of shelter on the side of your indoor enclosure just remember that they may try to climb on the roof so ensure that everything is safe.

Supply Shed

This can be built on the side of your goat shed or can be a completely separate building. It doesn't need to look amazing but it is helpful to have one nearby so that everything you need is to hand, making cleaning and taking care of your goats a lot easier.

The main things to include in your supply shed are:

Goat feed, for instance, alfalfa pellets and grain, keep them in water proof and rodent/pest proof containers.

Goat treats and supplements, such as sunflower seeds, baking soda and minerals.

Straw for bedding.

Leashes, brushes and hoof trimmers for general goat maintenance and care.

General 'work bucket' to hold any supplies you may need whilst working in your goat area.

If you are milking then you may want to keep any milking equipment in this shed too as well as wet wipes and antibacterial spray for cleaning udders before and after milking.

You may also want to keep your medicines in this supplies shed too if you do decide to keep some in stock. This is entirely up to you, I know of people that keep it in their store shed and others that keep them inside their house and I think it is dependent on your own preference as well as what you are choosing to keep in stock and the temperatures they need to be stored at as well as the temperature in your store shed and house. Many pet owners don't bother storing medicines because it is easier to just consult with the vet rather than try to diagnose and treat an illness by yourself but if you do store medicines then my advice is to read and follow the instructions on how to store correctly because they will last longer.

One suggestion I would make is to label up all your goat equipment so that you can find it easily when you need it. Whilst it is fine to just keep everything in their original packaging and throw it all in you may get irritated when you're having to search through piles of stuff just to find a packet of sunflower seeds. I've seen a lot of lovely supply sheds where everything has been placed in glass jars or plastic storage containers and labelled so that the owner just has to put their hand in and pull out what they need.
I would also advise that you lock up your goat shed both for the safety of any young children that may be in your house and also to prevent your goats from helping themselves.

Chapter 6: Goat Toys

Many people who are considering purchasing goats don't even think about goat toys, rather they picture these cute little creatures standing around on their lawn gazing thoughtfully at the fence, nibbling the grass and weeds here and there. An idyllic image BUT (and I can't stress this enough) your goat will not be happy just standing around in a field on your garden all day even with another goat or other farm animals for company and trust me a bored goat is a naughty goat and your new pet will soon get into trouble climbing the fence and trying to escape.

Goats are very intelligent creatures and as such get bored very easily. The good news is you can keep your new friends happy simply by buying a few cheap items for them to play with. If you are handy with a hammer and nails you could make exciting toys for them. It doesn't have to look pretty; your goat won't care as long as it's functional and interesting for them to play with.

A few goat toy ideas include:

Plastic or wooden children's playhouses – Your goat will love going in and out of these. One with ladders and slides will provide them with hours of entertainment but you can easily attach a few planks to make ramps for them to climb up and down if you wish to do so. Be aware that brand new these are often very expensive so I would recommend you buy second hand ones either via yard sales, car boot sales or on websites such as Gumtree, Craigslist, eBay or Facebook marketplace to name but a few.

Large Rocks – Great for climbing, arrange a few to make a 'rock playground' for your goat. The extra advantage of rock is that they will help wear down their hooves so you won't have to trim them as often.

Pallets or plastic crates – Again these can be great fun and you can either just stack them at various heights to make different sized platforms, put them together to make steps or keep them at similar heights and attach wooden planks between them to make bridges for your goats to walk from one to another. Many large companies or builder's yards will give used pallets away for free.

Large Tyres – For example tractor tyres or large car tyres are great toys for your Pygmy Goats. Stand them upright and half bury them in the ground and your goat will jump up and stand on top. Put a few together so they can climb and jump from one to the other.

Logs – These can be stacked into a pyramid to make a climbing toy or can be used to make ramps or bridges. Lay one down and attach a board to the top and you have a great seesaw.

Wooden Cable Spools – These are great platforms for your goats to climb on and if you want to make it into a kind of climbing frame for your goats you can do so by attaching wooden logs or planks to make bridges, slides and ramps. Again if you're lucky you may find them for free from electrical or DIY stores, energy and phone companies or even electricians.

Furniture – many people put out old tables, benches and even sofas and chairs for their goats to play on. Basically anything a goat can climb on will make a good toy. If you have a tree in your garden then placing a table or bench underneath will not only provide a place for your goat to lay down in the shade but they will also be able to climb up to nibble the lower branches as well as having fun simply jumping on and off. Again if you don't have any old ones of your own you can buy second hand or even make your own from any wood you have lying about.

Scratching Post – You can make these very cheap by buying a few scrubbing brushes and nailing them either onto a fence post or any large post set into the ground. Your goats will have great fun scratching their backs and heads on them.

Tether Ball – If you're in the UK then you may be more familiar with the term 'swing ball' but basically fix a large post in the ground and attach a ball to it with sturdy rope. Your goats will love head butting the ball to make it swing round.

Small Trampolines – goats will love to jump on and off these and may even have a nap or two on them.

Plastic Tunnels – Small goats love running through tunnels, you can combine them with platforms and pallets to make a great obstacle course for your new pets.

Other goat toy ideas are baby rattles attached to the fence, plastic children's slides, plastic barrels and empty children's paddling pools or sandboxes.

Goats are great jumpers and climbers which makes them incredibly fun to watch whilst they explore and play with their new toys. Just keep this in mind when setting up your goat playground however and always keep climbing toys in the centre of their fenced area because otherwise you may find they use their new platforms as a means of jumping over the fence!

If you only have a small garden then this may limit what you can provide for your goat however you can alternate toys on a weekly or fortnightly basis and this may prevent your goat from becoming bored as they will always have a variety of different things to keep them interested.

Always make sure the items you use are sturdy and 'goat proof', that is never give them anything they can destroy in a few minutes. You may need to replace items over time but things like wooden pallets, logs and plastic crates should be fairly sturdy and long lasting. Your goat may have a chew on some of their toys although they tend to prefer wood and natural items to plastic. If you are feeding them properly then they shouldn't eat things like tyres and hoses.

Do a quick online search for goat toys and you will find plenty of good photographs online to give you an idea of how to stack pallets or make bridges and platforms to keep your goats happy and occupied for years to come.

Remember you can pick up many of these items cheaply or for free. Don't be afraid to approach large companies and ask them if they reuse or recycle their pallets and wooden cable spools or if you can have them, the worst they can say is no but you will find that many don't have the storage space to keep them in order to reuse and they'll most likely be glad for you to take them off their hands.

Chapter 7: Common Illnesses

Like any living creature, goats are susceptible to a variety of illnesses. The good news is many of them are preventable as long as you understand how to correctly take care of your goat and provide them with suitable living conditions and a healthy, varied diet.

There may be other conditions not listed here that affect Pygmy Goats. For the purpose of this book I've listed the most common ones. Remember this section is just a guide, if you are worried at any time that your goat is ill then the best way to diagnose would be to consult a vet.

Enterotoxaemia
This is also known as the overeating disease and is caused by overeating. When the balance of bacteria in their rumens is disrupted a certain bacteria produces a poison which multiplies rapidly and makes the goat ill.

Symptoms
Symptoms include teeth grinding, high temperature or fever, water diarrhoea, sudden appetite loss, a swollen stomach or stomach pain which may result in the goat kicking their stomach, staggering about, crying out or lying on their side or looking depressed. Eventually they will be unable to stand and will lie on their side making paddling movements.

How To Treat
There is no effective cure and usually Enterotoxaemia is fatal. The only thing you can do is to consult your vet who may advise you euthanize your goat if there is nothing they can do.

Prevention
This is definitely a case of prevention is better than cure and the good news is you can avoid this disease completely. Introduce new foods slowly and don't allow too many treats. Lock up your feed store and make sure your goat cannot get into it at all. Feeding in

two halves twice daily and giving hay as free choice can reduce over feeding.

In some countries such as the US there is a vaccination that can prevent overeating so if you have a particularly greedy goat you may want to consider this but if you only have a couple of goats as backyard pets and you keep them in a dry area and don't over feed you can easily prevent this.

Worms
These are internal parasites that suck the blood of the goat internally, weakening their immune system which then makes them susceptible to other illnesses such as Pneumonia. If left untreated a goat can eventually die either from the worms themselves or from contracting a secondary illness. If your goat seems off the best thing to do first is to check for worms.

Symptoms
Symptoms include a dull coat, loss of appetite, pale gums, diarrhoea or stools that are clumped together, weight loss, lethargy and for lactating does, a drop in milk production.

The best way to get a diagnosis is to send a faeces sample to a vet but if you want to do a quick check at home then gently pull out the lower eyelid and check its colour. Worms suck the blood of the goat and therefore cause anaemia which is a low red blood cell count. Your goat's eyelids should be a rich salmon colour or bright pink. If it is pale pink or white then your goat probably has worms.

Treatment
The first thing to do is to de-worm your goat. Many people prefer to use organic de-worming products and whilst I can understand this I feel that if your goat already has a large number of worms that are making them sick then a chemical de-wormer usually works quicker. Usually with a chemical de-wormer you should give a second dose after eleven days in case there were any eggs missed during the first dose that will then have grown into adult worms.

As well as giving the de-wormer, provide a course of probiotics to help restore the natural balance to their rumens and start giving iron supplements until the red blood cell count is restored.

You may also want to consult a vet as they will be able to recommend the best products to use.

Prevention
A goat will always have a number of worms inside them, there's not really any way to prevent them however, when the numbers become very high it will start to make your goat sick. To keep the numbers low you have a choice as to whether to use a chemical de-wormer or an organic one made from herbs.
A chemical de-wormer is usually given twice a year although many people will say to rotate which ones you use because otherwise the worms can build up immunity. (If you do switch don't just change the brand, check the label to make sure the chemicals are different as you will find that many popular brands will contain the same ingredients).

If you are milking your goat then you will need to toss the milk after giving them a chemical de-wormer as it isn't safe to drink for a week. Many chemical de-wormers aren't suitable for pregnant goats either so always check the label.

A natural de-wormer is usually administered once a week to once a month.
A herbal de-wormer doesn't affect the milk at all so is a better option for pregnant or lactating does.

Feeding your goats hay and pumpkin is another way to keep worms at bay.

Having feeding equipment suspended from the ground so faeces cannot fall into it and cleaning your barn and garden on a regular basis can also prevent an infestation of worms.

For anyone who has a large amount of land for their goats then practice controlled grazing by giving them different parts of the pasture for them to graze on. However, for goats who are kept as back garden pets this isn't always possible therefore you should try to bring in foraged foods for them so they have new things to graze on because if they are grazing constantly on the same small patch of land the number of worms will increase making it more likely that they will constantly be suffering with them.

Pneumonia

Pneumonia is inflammation or an infection of the lungs and is used to describe a range of respiratory infections. It can quickly kill goats, especially young kids.

Symptoms

There are many symptoms of Pneumonia such as refusing food, hanging their heads, rapid or shallow breathing or laboured breathing signalled by their sides heaving. You may notice that your goat is listless, has a runny nose or nasal discharge. Sometimes your goat will sound congested or you may hear their chest rattling. Your goat will also develop a high fever. Pneumonia will eventually lead to death if left untreated.

How To Treat

If you suspect one of your goats has Pneumonia then you need to isolate them from the other immediately to stop it from spreading. To reduce the fever you should hydrate your goat. Antibacterial drugs such as Oxytetracycline can help but I would always seek advice from a qualified vet as well because a goat's lungs can rapidly fill up with fluid which can quickly kill them.

Prevention

Goats of any breed are highly susceptible to this disease however, the chances of them actually becoming ill with Pneumonia is generally low as long as their housing is well ventilated and free from draughts.

If you live in a particularly cold area then you may want to consider putting heat pads in your barn to keep your goats warm during winter.

Acidosis

This is when a goat's rumen PH becomes acidic and can occur if they accidentally ingest a high amount of concentrated food stuff like grain.

Symptoms

The goat may stagger about or have muscle twitching, hang their head or stare off into space for long period of time. Teeth grinding, bloating and swelling of the left flank are also symptoms of Acidosis.

Treatment

Try to neutralise the acid in their rumens by giving them something alkaline such as bicarbonate of soda. Stop access to food and provide them with smaller portions so that their rumens have time to rebalance.

As always contact the vet to get advice.

Prevention

Acidosis can make your goats ill and if you are only wanting a couple of goats as pets rather than running a farm you will want your goat to stay as healthy as possible rather than racking up high vet bills.

Acidosis is easy to avoid simply by providing a well-balanced diet that includes lots of hay as well as not overfeeding and not giving too much grain. Lock up your grain and food stores so that your goats cannot help themselves whenever they feel like it. Keep an eye on their intake of fresh spring grass if you have large pastures.

Also avoid sudden diet changes that may upset your goats' rumen and provide plenty of long stemmed fibre to keep their digestive tract healthy.

Caprine Arthritis Encephalitis (CAE)

This is a contagious viral disease and the main way it spreads is from mother to baby via colostrum or milk. It may also be spread amongst adult goats via bodily fluids or faeces if a goat is already infected.

Although it doesn't appear that CAE can be passed to humans some countries will still need you to report any cases of this to the relevant authorities so you should check the guidance on this online if your goat has contracted it. I believe it probably only affects those who are supplying goats milk to the general public but it is always better to make sure just to be on the safe side.

There are five main forms of CAE; Arthritis, Pneumonia, Mastitis, Encephalitis and Chronic Wasting.

Symptoms

Arthritic CAE – Symptoms include poor hair condition, reluctance to rise and /or walk, stiffness or swollen joints, weight loss, abnormal posture and sudden lameness. As the disease progresses you may notice your goat start to walk on their knees. Arthritic CAE is mostly seen in adults aged one to two years.

Pneumonic CAE – Symptoms include a chronic cough, weight loss and difficulty breathing.

Mastitic CAE – This only affects pregnant or lactating does and symptoms include decreased milk production coupled with a hard swollen udder.

Encephalitic – Lack of co-ordination, head tilt, blindness, depression, seizures, progressive paralysis and eventually death. This type of CAE is usually seen in kids of around two to four months old.

Chronic Wasting – This can be symptomatic of all types of CAE listed above. This is where the goat continues to lose weight even though there is no apparent loss of appetite.

Treatment
Whatever form it takes, CAE is a painful disease and unfortunately there is no specific treatment. Goats that contract this disease can be given care to support their condition such as pain medication and antibiotics to treat any bacterial infections that develop as a result but there is no known cure as such. Usually the kindest thing to do

with Encephalitic CAE is to euthanize your goat as no matter how much care is provided your goat will suffer and eventually die.

If you believe your goat is suffering from CAE then always contact a vet for advice.

Quarantine the infected goat and if any kids were nursing stop this immediately to prevent it spreading. Although this shouldn't be an issue if you only have a couple of goats as pets unless you did breed them, if this were the case you would need to have the kids tested just in case.

Prevention
As you are buying a couple of goats for pets then prevention is far better than ending up with high vet bills and sick animals. To avoid bringing CAE onto your land then you simply have to check that the goats you intend to purchase are free from CAE so always ask the breeder or owner before you buy. Anyone who is genuine will be happy to provide the results of the tests. However, make sure you don't just check the results for the goats you have purchased but for the whole herd. Personally I would want to see that all animals from this seller had been free for at least a year or two just to be on the safe side. Don't be afraid to ask if they have ever had any cases of CAE. It is definitely better to buy from someone who can explain about this disease rather than from someone who acts dumb about it or who genuinely hasn't heard of it.

Do not purchase a goat unless you are satisfied that a CAE test has been done and all the animals in the herd have had negative results.

A CAE test is a simple blood test and is relatively cheap so if you are in doubt then get a test done yourself via your vet.

If you have never had goats on your land before and those you purchase are CAE free then you should never have to worry about this if you are just keeping a couple as pets. Just remember that if one of your goats dies and you replace it or if you decide to breed or add to your herd then you should only introduce new goats onto your land if you have done a test. Any babies that are born should also be tested just to rule out any new genetic introductions that may have arisen.

Caseous Lymphadentitis (CL)

This is a disease caused by bacteria which results in abscesses which can be both external and internal and can eventually spread to the lungs and digestive tract.

It is highly contagious and is spread when an abscess bursts and another goat comes into contact with the pus.

Symptoms

Usually you will notice abscesses around the mouth or jaw, shoulder, neck, knees or upper leg.

If a goat has internal abscesses then you may notice excessive coughing.

Eventually the abscess will burst by itself, which is when it can be dangerous to other goats. If it is CL then the pus from the abscess will be greenish and odourless and may be lumpy rather than smooth. Humans may also be able to contract this disease if they come into contact with this pus, although it is extremely rare, I would still take precautions when handling a goat with CL especially if you have any cuts or open wounds. Wear gloves and always wash your hands after contact.

Treatment

If you believe one of your goats has CL then you should isolate them immediately and contact your vet who will take a sample of the pus and send it off for testing. They will also be able to provide up to date information on how to proceed should your goat test positive for CL. Assuming you take them before any abscesses burst then usually they will recommend that the abscess is properly lanced and cleaned – ideally by the vet rather than the owner - and the goat is then kept away from other goats for at least thirty days until the abscess is completely healed up as this way the infection cannot spread.

I will point out here that not all abscesses mean CL so you should go to the vet as soon as you spot any. If the vet says it isn't CL then you can use hot compresses and wait for them to rupture naturally rather than having the vet lance them. This will usually take up to a week and the abscess, once burst, should heal. The pus from a non CL abscess is usually white and smooth.

If you did have a lactating doe tested positive for CL then the milk should be pasteurised before being used regardless of whether it is being consumed by goat kids or humans. If the abscess was on the udder then the milk should be thrown immediately. Any kids that were feeding from the affected doe should be removed from her and bottle raised, I would also get them tested just to be certain it hasn't been passed on.

Prevention
Again this is another disease that shouldn't affect you as a pet owner as long as you ensure that the goats you purchase have been tested before you buy them. This is also another reason to visit a herd in person rather than buying without seeing because you will be able to check all the animals for abscesses so you can be confident that none of the goats the seller owns have this disease.

There are two CL vaccines available in some countries but there are side effects associated with each. It is also worth noting that once the vaccine has been given any subsequent tests will always be positive because the vaccine contains the bacteria that causes CL. Therefore when purchasing you should ask the seller if they have vaccinated against CL because this could be a reason for some or all of their animals testing positive. In my opinion if you are just owning a couple of goats as pets then you don't need to vaccinate because if your goat doesn't have it when they arrive on your property then they should never contract it unless you introduce new goats to them. Again, if you were ever replacing a goat you would need to have the test done before bringing the new ones onto your property. The vaccination is more appropriate for large herds, especially those that are being raised for breeding and milking purposes.

Johnes (Pronounced Yo-Knees) Disease

Johnes Disease is caused by a bacteria called Mycobacterium Avium Subspecies Paratuberculosis (MAP). It is a fatal gastrointestinal disease that is found in goats and other ruminants such as cattle, sheep, deer and so on.

The infection is contagious and is usually spread via the manure of the infected animal. MAP bacteria develops in the small intestine and is passed out via faeces. If these are swallowed with feed, grass, water or milk for instance, the healthy goat will be infected. If a doe is infected the disease can be present in her colostrum and milk which is why kids are very susceptible and unlike CAE, heat treatment on the milk isn't sufficient enough to kill the MAP organisms.

Usually once an owner discovers that one of their goats has Johnes Disease the rest of the herd have already become infected therefore if you suspect Johnes Disease in one goat you should isolate it and get every goat you own tested too as well as any other ruminant animals you may have.

Unfortunately, once the signs appear the goat will most likely already be at the end of life stage.

There is no vaccine as of yet that has been approved and sadly there is no cure. The best you can do is try to prevent Johnes Disease from being brought onto your property.

Symptoms

A goat can appear entirely healthy yet be infected with Johnes Disease and symptoms may not appear for a few months or even years later. This is why it's very important to ensure that the goats you buy have been tested and are free from the disease as are the others in the herd it was born into. Usually a goat will become infected within their first few months of life.

Symptoms can be vague and are similar to many other illnesses and include diarrhoea and rapid weight loss despite eating well. Eventually the goat will become thin and weak. In order to get a diagnosis you will need a lab test from a vet.

Prevention

As I mentioned there is no cure so therefore the best you can do is prevent it. The good news is if you are just buying a couple of goats as pets it is another case of as long as the goats have been tested beforehand and you are buying them from a Johnes Disease free herd there is no reason for you to ever worry about this disease.

Again if you introduce new goats or new ruminants onto your property you will need to get these tested as well before bringing them onto your land otherwise there is a risk of bringing the disease with them.

As tempting as it may be, don't ever let anybody bring goats or ruminants onto your land without making sure they have been tested and clear of Johnes Disease and don't take your goats to anyone else's property either unless you are sure that it is safe to do so.

You will most likely be feeding your goats whatever they can forage on your property as well as the goat feed and hay you bring in but if you do bring forage from other areas outside of your property then make sure it hasn't come from a place where other ruminants may have previously grazed just in case those animals had the disease. This is more a precaution than a serious concern because at the time of writing, free ranging ruminants such as deer or elk are thought to be free of the MAP infection and it is more apparent in those animals in captivity.

Practice good hygiene by keeping your goat areas as free of manure as possible and change bedding, water and feed regularly, especially if you notice faeces in it. Again, if you raise the feed equipment there shouldn't be a risk of this happening.

If you do have goats that are being milked or who have babies that they are feeding then try to clean the does' udders wherever possible before the kids nurse and before milking, as suckling or milking from manure stained teats can increase the risk of spreading the infection.

If you do have goats that are diagnosed with Johnes Disease don't immediately go out and buy more pet goats after they have passed on. The MAP organism is very hardy (they're rather like the cockroaches of the organism world) and can survive in the environment. It is resistant to damp, drying, heat and cold and whilst the majority will die out after several months without animals being present a few can remain for up to eleven months in soil and seventeen months in water, albeit in low levels. Therefore before purchasing more goats you would need to thoroughly wash and disinfect every part of your garden, goat shed, feeding equipment and water troughs several times and leave to dry out to ensure all the bacteria has definitely been eradicated. Just remember, if you wash out a water trough and feeding equipment, don't dump the slimy dirty water onto the ground as if there are organisms in there it will just infect the soil! I would recommend thoroughly disinfecting and leaving the area animal free for at least a year before bringing in any more pets just to be on the safe side.

There is plenty more information about keeping your goats healthy and Johnes Disease free but as this book is aimed purely at those people who are raising Pygmy Goats as pets I don't feel it necessary to go into any more detail. I'm confident that as long as you make certain you are buying goats from a herd that has been tested and is free from the disease then there is no reason why you should have to worry about it. I have included it here purely because I think it is important to understand why you should get your goats tested before bringing them onto your land and so you are aware of it but any more detail is probably not relevant unless you are keeping a large herd for milking or breeding purposes.

Bloat
This is when air bubbles form in the rumen and get trapped. It is usually caused by high quantities of unsuitable food, for instance eating too much grain or wet grass pastures which can cause frothy bloat.

Symptoms
Bloat is incredibly uncomfortable for a goat and you may notice them kicking their left side and grunting. Their left side will be hard and swollen and they will look a lot bigger than normal. Sometimes a goat will lie on their left side but this makes the condition worse because it traps the gas even more.

You may think that bloat sounds a lot like trapped wind in a human but it is a far more serious condition and can result in death if left untreated.

Treatment
To relieve the symptoms of bloat the air bubbles in the goat's rumen need to be broken down. You can help by massaging the goat's flank then trying to get them to walk about. If possible, elevate your goat on an incline so that their front legs are higher than their rear as this can help the gas escape.

Another option is to mix baking soda into your goat's feed as this can also take away bloat.

Some people recommend giving a vegetable oil and dish soap mixture if your goat is suffering from frothy bloat however other people disagree and believe that the vegetable oil will add to a goat's discomfort. If you believe that your goat has frothy bloat then mineral oil or milk of magnesia may be a better choice in breaking down the tiny bubbles in their rumen.

If none of these solutions work then you should contact a vet. They may prescribe a course of Penicillin or they may pass a tube into the goat's stomach in order to release the pressure in the rumen.

Prevention
Some goats may look bloated when in fact they simply have a full stomach but they should be able to pass wind or bring up cud easily. A goat with bloat will be in obvious discomfort and will appear distressed so if they look bloated but are happily chewing or playing then you shouldn't need to panic.

Bloat can usually be prevented by feeding a balanced diet, rationing their food and introducing new feeds gradually.

Urinary Calculi
This is a condition that affects male goats and is similar to Kidney Stones in a human. Crystals form in the urinary tract and block the flow of urine.

If the blockage isn't removed then the urine has nowhere to go and eventually causes the bladder to rupture, which will lead to death. It is a very painful condition and is one of the leading causes of death in male goats.

Symptoms
You may notice your goat is stretching and straining to urinate yet they either don't produce anything at all or only manage a few small dribbles. You may notice that any urine they do produce is dark in colour or contains blood. The goat may also act constipated or you may notice a swelling or discoloration of their penis.

Your goat may stand hunched over or may continually press their head against the fence or walls. They may moan or cry or look like they are in distress, especially when they are trying to urinate.

Other symptoms include shaking their head, a dull looking coat, white gums, shivering, worn out or hanging tail and teeth grinding.

Treatment
Unfortunately, treatment can be very challenging and isn't always successful unless it is caught early and treated immediately.

If your goat is straining but able to pass some urine then a drenching with an Ammonium Chloride solution can be enough to break up the tiny crystals.

There are other 'at home' remedies but because your goat can become ill very quickly I would always recommend that you treat these animals like you would any other pet and consult a vet before trying to cure your goat yourself.

Usually a surgical procedure is needed to release the blockage. The best case scenario is that the stones have collected in the end of the penis and can be snipped off. However, if the blockage is very severe and further up in the urinary tract then the surgical options can be very expensive and aren't always guaranteed to work. Even if the goat is cured the goat will have a higher chance of developing Urinary Calculi in the future.

If you believe your goat has Urinary Calculi then DO NOT force them to drink water. You cannot simply 'flush' it out and the more water they drink the quicker their bladder will fill up and eventually it will burst.

Prevention
Urinary Calculi is often caused by improper feeding. Calcium to Phosphorous Ratio of 2:1 in their food is important so you need to check everything you give them if you are buying store bought food and try to avoid too much grain.

Wethers are also prone to Urinary Calculi because castration stops testosterone being produced and this is the hormone that is responsible for the Urethra growing. If the males are castrated too early before their Urethra has time to grow then this can put them at risk of developing this condition. As a pet owner you probably won't be banding or getting your goat castrated unless you have bought a buck and then changed your mind, but you should check if you are buying a wether that they haven't been banded or castrated before 12 weeks of age.

Other reasons for Urinary Calculi include a low water intake; always make sure there is a fresh supply of water for your picky Pygmies, change this twice a day and offer warm water in the winter to encourage them to drink more.

Feeding Alfalfa hay and Lucerne can help, possibly because Alfalfa has a higher protein concentration and both are high in calcium.

Foot Scald and Foot Rot
Goats have a cloven hoof which means that their hooves are split in the centre. This space can trap manure, dirt and moisture where bacteria and fungus thrive. If a hoof becomes overgrown, the outer edges start to fold underneath and this can also then trap bacteria, which can lead to foot problems.

Symptoms
Foot Scald is the precursor to Foot Rot so the symptoms are very similar. Usually you will notice your goat lifting their leg up or limping because it is a painful condition. They may even stay on

their front knees to avoid putting any pressure on the hoof or hooves that are affected.

You may also notice a distinct and unpleasant odour coming from the foot.

Treatment
This includes soaking your goats' hooves in copper sulphate or zinc sulphate. You can also buy over the counter products if you have caught it early enough. Before treating you will need to trim the hoof first.

Prevention
Warm, wet weather conditions can make Foot Scald and Foot Rot develop quicker. The best way to prevent this condition is to keep your goats' feet trimmed regularly to avoid giving the bacteria and fungus a place to develop.

Coccidiosis
Coccidia are parasites that live and grow within the cells that line the gastro-intestinal tract. It is another disease that is transmitted if a goat eats faeces that are infected with the eggs of these parasites.

Symptoms
Symptoms will usually appear around five to thirteen days after contracting this disease. The main ones are loss of appetite, dehydration and weakness. You may notice that your goat has diarrhoea that may be bloody and dark but sometimes you may notice normal looking stools that smell foul. If this is left untreated the goat will eventually die.

Treatment
If you believe that your goat has Coccidiosis then you need to treat it immediately. Send a stool sample to your vet and ask for treatment. Usually drugs such as Baycox, Sulfa drugs, Amprolium and Decoquinate are prescribed.

Prevention
These parasites are always present in the environment so all goats will be infected with a small number but they do very little damage

unless it gets out of control. Adult goats usually have robust immune systems and so can resist an outbreak of Coccidia but young or sick goats can be affected as can those that are older or stressed.

The best way to prevent is to keep your goats' enclosure and barn as clean as possible, feed off the ground to prevent them accidentally eating faeces with their food, making sure your feeders and water troughs are cleaned regularly and any faeces are removed promptly and keeping your goats as happy and stress free as possible. If you believe any of your goats are infected then separate them from the rest until they have been completely treated, especially if there are any baby kids or older goats on the property.

Common Goat Behaviour
Pygmy Goats are energetic and playful yet can be happy spending a lot of time in one spot, so if you see them sat for long periods it doesn't necessarily mean that they are sick and this on its own shouldn't be a cause for concern.

Your goats should enjoy playing together and being in each other's company. A sick goat will often isolate itself.
These animals tend to be fairly quiet and whilst some can be noisy, in general they don't tend to cry a lot (unless you only have one lone goat!) other than the odd bleat now and then. If you listen carefully to your goat, eventually you should be able to distinguish between a normal 'happy' bleat and one that is distressed. For example, your goat may bleat when it is hungry or you may notice your goat bleating in hot weather because it is thirsty. Usually these bleats start off quiet and become louder over time.

A healthy bleat may sound 'livelier' whereas a goat that is in pain will have a different tone; much like a human who is in pain will have a different cry to one who isn't.

Talk to the breeder when you purchase your goat as they may be able to provide information on the goat's behaviour and noises.

Signs Of A Sick Goat
Other than a different tone when bleating and isolating themselves from their friends there are other signs you can look out for:

68

- Teeth Grinding
- Diarrhoea or faeces that aren't 'normal'
- Difficulty urinating or showing pain when trying to urinate
- Bloated or hard stomach
- Lack of interest in drinking or refusing to drink
- Lack of interest in food or refusing to eat
- High temperature – anything above 38.6 degrees Celsius/101.5 degrees Fahrenheit is classed as a subnormal temperature. A temperature of 39.7 degrees Celsius/103.5 degrees Fahrenheit or above is a fever
- Pressing their head against fences or walls
- Kicking or biting their stomach
- Head shaking
- Green or cloudy nasal discharge
- Rapid breathing or abnormally slow breathing
- Pale or grey eyelids
- Standing hunched over
- Lying on their side or not moving for hours on end
- Weight loss without a loss in appetite

Should I Call A Vet?

If you are a farmer and are experienced with animals then there may be some things you can do yourself at home, however as a pet owner you should treat these animals as you would a dog or a cat so my advice would always be that if you suspect your goat is ill then consult with a vet, especially if your goat is isolating itself, lying down in one spot for hours on end, appears lifeless or is moaning in pain.

Vet bills can be expensive, especially as you will need one who specialises in livestock so it may be wise to see if it is possible to get your goat insured or to put away money in a savings account, as this way you will be paying out small amounts each month rather than having to fork out a large lump sum if your goat does get sick for any reason.

Chapter 8: Goat Shows

Why Show A Goat?

As a pet owner taking your animal to a show can be great fun, kind of like beauty pageants for goats.

Attending these shows are a good way for you to share your hobby with others who have a love of goats because you will meet many breeders and owners that you can talk to and share anecdotes and care tips and if you are in any doubt about how to care for your beloved pet you can ask questions - most people will love the chance to share their knowledge.

Some judges will talk to you individually after a show so you can get advice on why your goat didn't win (if this is the case) or how you can improve next time.

As well as learning about what makes a 'good' Pygmy Goat, shows are also beneficial as they often gain publicity which encourages breeders to continually breed only the best animals and strive to continually improve bloodlines. Anyone who breeds and enters animals in the shows can gain recognition this way which makes it easier to sell their goats in the future so if you were going to breed, whether it be to make money or just so you are provided with a natural source of milk, then it may be worth considering attending goat shows as a way of advertising your animals and building up a reputation in the goat world.

If you don't want to breed you can still make connections with those that do; should you ever want a new goat either to make your herd bigger or to replace one that dies then by attending shows you will be better placed at finding a breeder with excellent animals.

Height Restrictions

Pygmy Goats are genetically dwarfed and Pygmy Goat clubs will have their own rules with regards to height. For males the maximum height at the withers is approximately 56cm (22 inches), less for females.

Make sure you have measured and ascertained that they are the correct height before you attend the show otherwise you may be disqualified.

They must have short legs and cobby bodies. They can be any colour except completely white or have white Swiss markings on the face.

Before showing

There are shows held at various venues across the country, some are part of larger agricultural shows whilst others are run by club members and are held on smaller sites. There are often forms to fill out in order to register your goat for a show so I would advise you find all the shows that you would like to attend for the year, list them in date order and request all the paperwork early so you are able to get it sent back before the deadline. Read everything carefully so you understand exactly what classes are available and are suitable for you and your goat. The dates and venues are usually listed on the club's websites as well as printed in their magazines or newsletters.

Your goats will have to be registered and you usually have to be a member of a club in order to take part in a show for the breed section classes. Check that the goat(s) you want to show don't have any faults which will disqualify them such as faults with their teats or mouth defects. Those which don't qualify or which aren't registered can be entered into pet classes. These are more informal, usually kids enter, but the goats will still be judged on confirmation, condition, presentation and temperament and rosettes will be awarded to the winners.

These groups will have their own set of guidelines and rules to follow as well as those of the show so make sure you are accustomed with all of these before you attend otherwise you could be disqualified.

Some shows may run over two days so these may not be appropriate if you are travelling a long way as you would have to find somewhere for both you and your goat to stay overnight.

What About Me?

Technically the judge should be judging your goat and not you. However, you should try to be as professional as possible as this will always go in your favour. The judge will warm to you more if you are taking the show seriously rather than larking about in the show ring.

Some open shows, or those that are part of a larger agricultural show, may be flexible about their dress code but you should always check if this is required when you sign up for the show as you may be required to wear 'show whites' which will either be a white coat or a clean white top and clean white trousers depending on where you live. The colour has been chosen so as not to detract from the goats so if you there aren't any rules on what to wear, try to choose something light in colour and plain rather than patterned.

If you are taking part in a US 4H show then please note that these are very strict about proper show attire.

As Pygmy Goats are so small you will most likely be bending down a lot in order to square them up and hold them in position. For a show you will need to crouch down with your knees bent but not physically touching the ground. This may take a while to get used to so I would probably practice this at home first.

Attitude

Don't go into a show expecting to win; without wanting to sound condescending it is highly unlikely that you will win the grand prize on your first show, however this doesn't mean you have to go in with a defeatist attitude either.

Both you and your goat will be nervous, which is entirely normal so take part with the attitude that you are both there to gain experience and to have fun, that way if you don't win anything you won't be too disappointed.

If you don't place as high as you'd hoped (or if you don't place at all) don't feel upset, take on board the judge's comments and if possible talk to them after the show to find out how you can improve for future competitions.

If you're not sure what you are doing pretend that you do and copy the person in front. Try to act confident even if you don't necessarily feel it; stand tall, hold your head up high and smile. Not only will you impress the judges but it may help your goat to relax and be confident too.

Illnesses

Most shows should ask for proof that the goats have been CAE, CL and Johnes Disease tested but there are plenty of other illnesses that goats may have and whilst it shouldn't happen let's be realistic; people will show sick goats. You may not be able to tell that they are ill by looking at them and their owners may not even be aware of it but think very carefully before showing your pet as there is always a chance they could catch a serious disease.

There are precautions that can be taken such as having a portable pen that you only use for shows or putting disposable tarpaulin or plastic sheets on the ground before placing bedding on them. You can even put tarpaulin between the pens so that your goat doesn't have direct contact with other goats whilst they are waiting to take part. However, they are going to have to mix with other goats in the ring so there is no way you can make sure they are one hundred percent safe; it is more about limiting the amount of exposure they have with others.

If you are worried you can send your goat(s) to be tested after a show to ensure they haven't picked up any infection.

Preparation

Grooming

You don't necessarily *have* to bath, clip and brush your goat for a show BUT it may reduce your chances of winning if you don't. Although judges award points for conformation if your goat shows up muddy with unkempt hair and overgrown hooves whilst others are immaculately groomed, the judge will most likely look more favourably on them. If nothing else you want your goat to look well cared for.

Clipping a Pygmy Goat may be a challenge if you haven't done it before but the more you practice the easier it becomes. There are lots of videos online that you can watch to see how it's done. Clipping your goat makes them look neat and tidy but you can also highlight certain traits, for example, you can emphasize their leg muscles by trimming their legs if they have a thick layer of hair.

I would advise you clip two to three weeks prior to a show as this will give you a chance to tidy up any areas you may have missed and also allows any bad lines to grow out.

Hooves should always be trimmed and cleaned two days before a show.

Brush your goat every day for at least two weeks prior to a show.

Many owners will bathe their goat before taking them to a show which is fine but be sure to use a suitable, good quality animal shampoo and rinse thoroughly to get all the soap out otherwise it could irritate your goat's skin and can make the coat dull rather than shiny.

On the day of the show you can make their hooves and horns shine by rubbing on a little Vaseline or hoof oil. If your goat doesn't have horns you can still rub their buds or scurs to make those shine instead.

Handling
You will need to walk your goat around the showing arena so you will need to get them used to this beforehand. A goat that is only handled for shows may struggle or freeze once they are in the show ring because they are not used to it. To a judge (and other owners) this can look like you don't have control of your goat.

The best way to do this is to make it a part of their everyday life by walking them around your garden as much as possible using a show collar just like you would in a show. Just a short walk in a circle around their pen or barn is a good way to get them to feel comfortable. Teach them to walk and stand quietly on the leash. Remember the new surroundings of a show will be stressful enough

74

for your goat so the more you can get them used to what is expected of them beforehand the better.

Standing
As well as walking your goat you will also be expected to correctly position them whenever the judge asks you to so that they can check their conformation and compare them to others taking part. Again this should be practiced beforehand not only so that your goat can get used to you touching their legs and standing them in a certain way but also to give you the confidence to quickly and easily adjust them whenever necessary.

When positioned their back should be nice and straight with their back legs under their hips and their front legs under their shoulders. Their neck should be extended and their head should remain steady.

To position, put your hand under their chest at the front and lift until their feet are off the ground. When you put the goat back down their feet should be level and apart but not splayed.

Run your hand down their back until you reach their hips and lightly press whilst rocking your hand from side to side at the same time; this should move their hind legs back and apart.

To get your goat used to the judges, let someone you know handle your goat and run their hands along their back so that they can get used to other people touching them as well as you. This should make them less skittish when they attend shows.

Another thing to practice is opening your goat's mouth whilst holding their lead because you will need to do this so that they judge can inspect their bite.

Talking quietly to your goat throughout their training and then during the shows can reassure and help calm them quicker if they are a little bit nervous in the ring.

What Should I Take?
The main things you will need at a show are a show collar and lead, a water bucket, feed and a bowl to put it in, hay – a hook on hay rack is also a good idea so that they don't have to eat directly from the ground – and a brush or comb so that you can groom your goat before they are called.

Most shows will provide bedding but I would always check this beforehand just to make sure as you want your goat to be comfortable the whole time they are there.

You should also take a safety pin or a clip as you will be given a goat number to pin on yourself.

Moving
In the UK, DEFRA movement regulations means that you are not allowed to move a goat unless you have an Animal Movement License. This means if you want to take your goat to a show you will need one of these licenses for both the journey there and the journey back. Other countries will also require something similar because these animals are classed as livestock so make sure you fill these out in advance because the Show Secretary will usually ask to see it on the day.

These can usually be done online but if you prefer you may also be able to obtain a paper copy.

On The Day
Upon arrival you should find the Show Secretary and hand in all your paperwork. They will check everything is in order, complete

any sections that apply to them and then hand you back the relevant documents that you need. They should then hand you a show number to wear on your clothes and direct you to your pen.

Settle your goat in their pen with food and water. Usually there should be some show organisers milling about who will be happy to show you where you can fill up your water bucket. Whilst you wait for your class to be called you should have time for any last minute grooming. You may wish to spray on some coat conditioner to give their coat a silky shine.

Listen carefully for your class to be called. The steward or judge should show you where to stand and how to line up so– usually it will be in numerical order.

How a show is organised is at the judge's discretion on the day so each one may be different but they usually follow the same pattern.

To start with you will be asked to line up with the goat's rumps facing the judge so they can do their inspection first. Listen carefully to all instructions and copy what everyone else is doing.

The judge will usually walk along the line to assess each one and then will examine each goat individually. This inspection will consist of seeing the 'bite', looking at the feet and checking for any teat faults. During this time you will be expected to keep your goat as still as possible.

The judge will then ask you to walk your goat in a straight line, away and then back towards them, often this is done in pairs so that they can compare your goat to another. Once you have done this you may be asked to stand your goat facing either to the right or to the left so that they can look at their profile.

Once everyone has been examined you will be asked to walk in a circle so the judge can see how each goat moves and then each goat will be lined up facing the opposite direction to the one in which they started.

Whenever your goat is stood in a line up you should ensure that they are positioned correctly with their legs apart, back straight and head held high as this will help the judge to see their conformation and make their decision.

At the end you may be asked to move into a line according to placement. Don't get too elated or upset early on as you may be asked to move again if the judge changes their mind so listen carefully for your number just in case you are asked to swap places.

Once the judge is satisfied with their decision the rosettes will be given out and the judge will explain the reasons for why each goat placed as they did. If you aren't as high as you wanted or you don't place you can learn what to improve upon in the future.

First place winners from each class will compete at the end for 'best in show' or 'grand champion'.

Tips

Always check the rules and regulations for your show before you attend – there's nothing worse than travelling miles for a show only to find you are disqualified because your animal doesn't meet the right criteria.

There are lots of videos online that are helpful to watch to give you an idea of what is expected of you and your goat but actually watching a show in person may be more beneficial so it is recommended that you attend at least one or two shows before you take part.

Practice walking and standing before a show because even the most well behaved goat may end up having 'stage fright' on the day. Remember they are in a completely different environment to what they are used to at home. Practicing before a show gets them used to what is required of them so this at least can be familiar and not as frightening.

Trim their hooves so that the judge can see that your goat can walk correctly and doesn't have any defects. Always comb and clip your goat according to goat standards.

Dress appropriately yourself. If you are required to wear certain clothes then do. Whilst you shouldn't be disqualified for wearing the wrong attire it certainly won't help you make a good impression.

Always keep your goat between you and the judge; if the judge is at the goat's rear you should stand at the front. As the judge moves around to the right and towards the goat's front you should step round to stand on the left hand side of the goat. This prevents you from getting in the judge's way or blocking their view.

Make sure there is enough room between your goat and the goat in front; the last thing you want is to get disqualified because your goat has nipped another goat's rump!

Keep an eye on the judge at all times as they will tell you what they would like you to do. They may also ask you questions, which you may miss if you aren't paying attention.

Don't ever talk to the person next to you. This is considered very rude and can distract the judge. The whole time you are in the ring you should be focused on the judge and your goat.

Always remain calm. Your goat - whilst a pet and possibly in your eyes a member of your family - is also an animal and they won't always behave the way you want them too. This can be frustrating but try not to get worked up and lose your temper, never shout, hit or treat your goat roughly. Remember your goat may be scared, bored or just in a mood and getting worked up won't help. Show that you aren't phased by their bad behaviour by remaining calm. This will make you seem professional and will go in your favour.

Always be a good winner or a good loser. There's nothing worse than someone who sulks or storms off just because their goat hasn't placed high. However disappointed you may feel on the inside, don't let it show. Take time to congratulate the winners and those who placed ahead of you. Take all comments on board so that you can improve for future shows.

Chapter 9: Horns

There are many controversial topics when it comes to goats and as silly as it sounds, horns are at the top of the list with each owner having their own opinions.

Some will say that the horns are natural and should be kept intact whilst others will say they are the mark of the devil and should be removed as soon as possible!

Whilst I do have my own opinion on horns I'm not here to tell you what you should or shouldn't do and it is entirely up to you, as a goat owner, on what your preference is. I will give you the arguments for and against horns as well as information on how to remove them but the final decision is up to you.

Should I Keep My Goats' Horns?
A common argument for keeping horns is that they protect goats from predators and are their only defence mechanism. To me this is a myth. Firstly, goats are prey animals in the wild, which means that many creatures will hunt them for food. Goats have a 'flight or fight' instinct and most of the time they would prefer to run rather than fight. If cornered then yes they would use their horns to defend themselves but, as sad as it is, the majority of the time this won't save them, not in the wild and not in your back garden.

As an owner YOU are the one who is responsible for your goats being safe from predators and this is done with a secure fence and shed not horns so if your reason for keeping your goats' horns is to keep them safe then get rid of them. Trust me, horns will most likely do your goat (and the rest of the household) more harm than good.

I will point out here that I do think horns look great BUT I don't believe that just because they may be more aesthetically pleasing they should be left on a domesticated goat....I also happen to think that Pygmy Goats look just as cute without the horns!

My opinion, based on my personal experiences and in depth research is that goats in captivity, even little tiny ones like these, should not be kept with their horns.

The reasons for this are as follows:

Firstly, although they may well be natural, horns can cause a goat a lot of problems. Yes, if they are wild goats living out in natural habitat they are not going to encounter fences and other obstacles...as a pet they are going to have limited space and be fenced in every single day and, as I mentioned before, goats are inquisitive and they will most likely try to escape on a daily basis and horns do not aid this. In fact, horns can be very detrimental even to a goat that isn't trying to escape. They can get caught on fences, feeders and a number of other things and a goat doesn't understand how to dip the end of their horns back down to pass back through the hole and therefore they end up getting stuck.

You may think this might be cute and if you're around twenty four seven and happen to catch them doing this then yes, I can see how a goat who has it's horn stuck in a fence can be cute, you snap a quick picture and set them free, what's the harm? However, if you happen to be out for long periods of time and are not around when the goat gets themselves stuck they can end up being seriously injured or even killed. Even if they stand perfectly still (which is not very realistic, if they're caught they are going to panic) they are an easy target for prey if they are stuck and can't escape.

It is true that a goat without horns can still get their head stuck but horns are just an extra liability.

Aside from getting stuck, horns can get damaged and this can be very painful for a goat. Given the fact that you should always have a minimum of two goats, horns can easily be broken off through fighting or playing and if they are pulled off completely there can be an open wound which can bleed – a lot! This is because once they are fully grown these horns will contain blood vessels.

As well as accidentally injuring each other your goat(s) may use their horns as a weapon which can not only damage their own horns

81

but that of their playmates too. You will often see two goats head butting each other but sometimes a goat will run into the other ones side rather than rushing it head on. They may then suddenly jerk their head backwards and up. This movement with horns can cause serious damage.

Thirdly, you should consider your own safety and that of others in your household or visitors. Whilst you shouldn't allow your goats to get into the habit of head butting you anyway, even when young, if they head butt you and they have horns it can be incredibly painful!

Remember that these animals are livestock and they don't have to be on the attack to cause damage. When feeding, watering, trimming hooves, petting, bathing, grooming, milking and all the other number of things you will do to care for your pet, you will be in close proximity to their heads. You could be bent down to give them a cuddle, they move their head the wrong way and you've lost an eye!

If you have children that live with you or just have friends and relatives that visit with kids, then horns are a definite NO! One wrong move by a child or a goat (and believe me, both are unpredictable!) and you have a badly injured child!

If you are milking your goats then you will need to use a milking stand and horns aren't accommodated for on these contraptions which means you will need a set up that allows you to milk safely whether this is buying a custom built stand or making one yourself – either way it could be more costly and inconvenient than simply getting rid of your goats' horns to begin with.

I think that you should also consider what the future will hold for your goat. In an ideal world you will keep them for the whole of their lives BUT if your circumstances change and you end up having to sell your goats then the chances of rehoming them are considerably lower if they have horns because – for all the reasons given above – most people do not want a goat that has intact horns.

A non-safety reason for keeping horns is that they are necessary to regulate your goat's body temperature but I don't agree with this.

I'm not disputing the fact that horns aren't vascular, which means they can give out heat, plenty of research has proven that goats in desert climates have longer horns with a thinner outer layer which allows for more heat to be released whereas those goats living in cooler climates have smaller, thicker horns to prevent too much heat being released.

What I do dispute is that goats DON'T NEED their horns to regulate their body temperatures because if this were true then in the summer all those goats that were naturally polled, disbudded or banded would be dying as soon as the hot weather hit. If horns were needed to regulate body heat then naturally polled goats wouldn't exist because the goats used to reproduce the gene that eliminates horns wouldn't have been able to mate and give birth if they were dying from heat exhaustion so whilst I agree with the fact that horns can help with regulating the body temperature of a goat, I don't believe this their horns are the only way they do this.

The opposite must also be true too; that in colder weather the heat must still be lost via the horns in winter and therefore it can make your goat colder in winter.

Another reason given for keeping horns is that getting rid of them is a non-medical and unnatural procedure. However, there are many things we do to our pet goats that are non-medical and aren't natural – castration for one, also tattooing and ear branding, injections to prevent certain illnesses and so on. All of these actions cause some level of pain and discomfort for a short period of time and removing horns is no different. The long-term benefits outweigh the short-term discomforts and it is not a cruel or mean thing to do.

So what options do you have for getting rid of horns? It is either disbudding, banding or having them surgically removed. I will go through each option individually.

Disbudding

The Procedure

This is the safest, fastest and most humane way to remove horns. It is done when the goats are very young, before the horns even start to grow, so they will very quickly forget about it.

A very (very!) hot disbudding iron is used to burn off the horn bud killing the tissue so that the horn cannot grow. This specially made iron sterilizes and cauterizes the area so that there is no bleeding and a minimal risk of infection. Whilst it is painful the whole process from start to finish only lasts about twenty seconds. As soon as it is over with the goats are usually straight back to nursing or drinking a bottle.

Occasionally, mild localized swelling can occur but this is very rare.

Scabs fall off after approximately two to four weeks and the hair will grow back soon after.

I'm not going to go into the details of how to disbud because most responsible breeders would not sell a goat with horns as a pet for all the reasons listed above and so disbudding should ideally be done before you take your new goat home. The other reason for having the breeder do it is that the baby can then run straight back to its mom to nurse.

If you are breeding your own goats then feel for the goat buds when born and check every day. Male buds will grow faster than females because of their hormone levels but it is usually around three to ten days when they appear.

If you did wish to learn how to disbud because you have decided to breed your pets then there are plenty of videos online, however I believe that if you are only keeping a couple of goats as pets as opposed to running a farm with dozens of them then you don't really need to know how to do it yourself because you should be able to pay somebody to do it for you. Also, it needs to be done properly; if the iron is held on too long it can cause brain damage, if it isn't held on long enough then scurs can occur. Done incorrectly it can cause problems for your goat later in life.

Not all vets will disbud but if you can find another goat owner living nearby who is experienced they may charge you a nominal fee, around £10 in the UK or $5-$10 dollars in the USA depending on your location.

Scurs

These occur when the horn tissue isn't properly burned away so the leftover tissue continues to grow over time. They can come in all shapes and sizes and most of the time they just look unsightly, like deformed horns, but you will need to keep an eye on them as they can break easier than the original horns would have, causing blood loss, open wounds and can lead to infection if left untreated.

Sometimes scurs can grow backwards and curl towards the head – if this happens they need to be removed by a vet.

Banding

For older goats that haven't been disbudded, horns can be banded with castration bands. You can purchase these online although I would always recommend that as a pet owner you consult a vet.

The Procedure

The band is placed at the base of the horn. For the first couple of hours it will annoy the goat causing them to thrash about trying to knock it off. After a few hours the 'feeling' in the horn will be lost - kind of like if you tied an elastic band really tightly around your finger. At this point the goat will appear oblivious and as an owner you will think the worst is over. However, the band will then begin to cut off the blood supply and this is when it becomes VERY PAINFUL for the goat.

Eventually the goat will be in a lot of pain and will become too frightened to move because whenever they do the horn will wiggle. They will avoid their playmates and possibly even their humans and they will most likely stop eating.

This is a risky stage because if the horn falls off before the blood supply is fully stopped and the horn is dead the goat will bleed a LOT. If you are not around to help them then they could potentially die. Of course that is the worst case scenario and if all goes well there will be minimal blood loss.

The whole process takes around four to six weeks from banding the horn to it falling off plus another two to three weeks for it to completely heal.

Whilst it may sound like a relatively simple procedure many owners will avoid banding horns. As well as it being painful, stressful and risky your goat will become distrustful of you and won't want you near their head for a very, very long time. They may even avoid you altogether and if these goats are your pets it can be sad to find that they are no longer playful towards you. If you had a tame and friendly goat it may take you a long time to get them back to the sweet natured loving creature they were before the banding.

If your goats have horns that are causing damage, constantly getting caught on fences, being used to bully other goats or to terrorise you and your family then banding is the best alternative if they are too old to disbud but if you buy your goats from babies rather than older ones then I would urge you to either buy ones that have been disbudded or are naturally polled.

Surgery
You can have a vet remove the horns from an older goat but not only is this costly but it is also a major surgical procedure. Goats don't do well under anesthetic so they may not even survive the operation but if they do it is not very nice at all.

The Procedure
The vet will put your goat to sleep and then cut out the horn buds. This procedure will leave an open wound leading into the goat's nasal cavity. Afterwards there will be lots of drainage and oozing from the site and you will need to change their bandages on a daily basis.

Remember that these animals are livestock and live outdoors and no matter how much you clean their sheds and outdoor area they are going to be urinating and defecating so an open wound will put them at a high risk of infection.

Again this is a risky, stressful and painful procedure and should only be done if it is your only option.

Can I Cut My Goat's Horns Or Scurs Off?

If you are wondering if you can just cut your goats horns off with a saw or other sharp instrument the answer is NO!

I believe many people think goats' horns are like human finger nails or hair as in you don't really feel them and if someone cuts them you barely even notice. Goats' horns however aren't like this at all, there are major arteries running through them and even scurs will contain blood vessels so rather than comparing it to someone trimming your nails you should compare it to someone chopping off your arm…without anaesthetic!

Cutting a goat's horns off is painful and inhumane and I do not recommend it at all. The goat will start to bleed heavily and if this isn't stopped immediately they will bleed to death in a matter of minutes. Stopping a Pygmy Goat from bleeding will not be as easy as you think either, despite their small size because they will be thrashing around and you will need to put a huge amount of pressure on to stop the blood flow.

So no, chopping off your goats' horns yourself is not an option!

Polled

A goat that is born hornless is known as polled. You will be able to feel two rounded bumps on their head but their horns will never appear.

Breeders can ensure that goats don't have horns by breeding those with the polled gene. An easy way to explain it is to say that goat DNA has two slots for the horn gene. One slot gets filled by the mother and one by the father. If two goats are bred and they both have the horn gene then the babies that are born will have horns. Likewise if both parents have the polled gene then the kids will have

87

no horns. If, however, one parent has the horned gene and one parent has the polled gene then any kids that they have will be given both the horn gene and the polled gene. The horned gene is recessive and the polled gene is dominant so in this case the babies will be born polled.

Being born polled means that they don't need to be disbudded and as nobody really likes the disbudding process one wonders why more breeders don't breed polled goats. The reason is this; at one point there were lots of polled goats in the USA but in the 1940's a report was published which stated that breeding polled goats increases the risk of the babies being hermaphrodites – meaning that they have both male and female reproductive organs and are sterile so they couldn't be bred. Many breeders stopped breeding polled goats whilst others stopped registering their polled goats or tried to disguise them as being disbudded.

Whilst breeding specific traits in any animals comes with health risks it is worth noting that not enough research has been done into this when it comes to breeding Pygmy Goats to be polled and I don't believe there is enough evidence to say whether it should be done or not.

Some breeders believe that it is fine as long as two polled goats aren't bred together whilst others have bred polled to polled and say that the risk of them having sterile babies is no higher than when breeding those with horns.

If you don't want to disbud or band but you don't want horns then it may be worth looking for a breeder that offers polled Pygmy Goats. As long as you do the usual health checks as you would with any other animal then you shouldn't have any problems. The only downside is that because there are not as many breeders out there for the reasons explained above you may find it difficult to find any in your area which may mean travelling further afield for your new pets.

Conclusion

Whether you keep your goats' horns or not is entirely up to you. The aim of this chapter is to provide you with the necessary information so you can make an informed decision.

I would consider whether you really want to be ducking and diving to avoid horns or do you want a pet that you can cuddle? All too often pet goats end up being rehomed, locked up or tied to fence posts because their owner has realized that their cuddly pet is too dangerous even when they're being friendly. Even small Pygmy Goats can do serious damage with their horns.

Whilst I personally wouldn't keep a goat with horns as a pet I do understand why many want to. Just remember though that if you decided to get rid of your goats' horns in the future it can be more painful, stressful and dangerous the older the animal is so if you are in two minds I would recommend to just buy them without horns.

Chapter 10: Breeding

As this book is focusing on Pygmy Goats as pets you most likely won't want to breed however, some pet owners do eventually decide to breed their animals and therefore this chapter has been included just in case.

Why Breed?

There are many reasons why pet owners decide to breed their goats. The first reason is that they are so darn cute that they decide they want more! I think this is a great reason but is one that needs to be considered carefully from a space and financial point of view.

A second reason for breeding is if your pets are your hobby as breeding is one more facet to this and provides hands on experience with caring for a goat through pregnancy as well as rearing the babies from birth and for an animal lover this can be an incredibly exciting experience.

Thirdly, people will breed their goats because they wish to make money from selling babies however I will warn you now this isn't the money spinner a lot of people believe it to be. Some people do make money from selling their babies but at the time of writing many owners are reporting that their goats are not selling and they are having to sell them cheaply because they don't have the space for them. Therefore, I would think very carefully about breeding if you are only doing so to make money.

Pygmy Goats are not usually purchased to be milked, possibly because their milking period is only between 120-180 days a year which is a lot shorter than other dairy breeds and they only produce one to two quarts a day on average. Having said this their milk is high in butterfat and delicious and many of those who are lactose intolerant or allergic to cows' milk find that they can drink goats' milk without any issues. This is another reason for pet owners to decide to breed, because they wish to milk their goats. Just remember if you milk you should do so for your own personal consumption because if you plan to sell to the public you will need a license to do so.

Whatever your reason is for breeding I urge you to consider the practicalities. It is not cheap as you will have to buy extra food, adjust your doe's diet plus feed and care for the babies when they arrive.

Not only will your food bills increase but have you got the space to keep your original goats plus the babies? Sometimes one pregnancy can result in three to four kids or more. Even if you are planning on selling the babies you won't be able to do this immediately as you need to wean them first and make sure they are all healthy plus it will take time for you to find good homes for them to go to. Please be a responsible breeder and consider not only your reasons for breeding but what will happen afterwards and put a plan in place before you put your doe with a buck.

Should I Breed Unregistered Goats?

Okay so you have enough space and can afford to keep the babies until they are old enough to go to new homes. The next thing you need to consider is whether you are breeding registered award winning show goats or fabulous milking stock?

If the goat you are planning to breed isn't registered then I would be tempted not to breed. To me it's kind of like the difference between breeding a mongrel or a pedigree dog; if you are going to breed, only breed the best.

Ideally when breeding you should be aiming to strengthen and improve the bloodline, secondly, although I mentioned above that selling baby goats can be difficult, it is far easier if the goats are registered and you can have the added selling point of them being show goats or high quality milking stock as well as just amazing pets.

When Can A Female Be Bred?

Pygmy Goats can be fertile from around two months but that doesn't mean that they should be bred at this age just that if you leave your female and males together then a pregnancy could occur. This is why bucks should be separated from the does at a very young age.

Ideally a female doe should be around eighteen months of age when you breed her. This means that she should be around two years old when she gives birth and ensures that she is fully grown, strong and healthy and mature enough for this.

A male goat can be used for breeding from around seven months of age although again leaving him until he is a year or older means he's more likely to be ready for the task in hand.

To get the healthiest kids you should only breed the healthiest animals. The doe should be healthy and a good weight before breeding. Make sure she is free from parasites and has had her vaccinations. Also drench her with a de-worming product before mating.

As well as being a suitable age it is vital that your female Pygmy Goat is not over weight because goats store fat internally around their vital organs including the uterus, which means there isn't as much space available for their uterus to grow during foetal development which can lead to difficult births.

As well as being healthy and a good weight your females should have good conformation and should be from well-established bloodlines. Ideally you would start your breeding journey by using a doe that has already given birth a couple of times without issues but of course if you have bought a couple of females for pets and have decided at a later date that you want to breed them then this may not be possible. Whatever the reasons for breeding and the age of your does you should find out as much about their family history as possible; has the mother had any breeding difficulties? Also look at their father and see if any of his stock has had any breeding difficulties in the past as problems can be inherited from both sides.

If you have never bred goats before – and I am assuming that as you have bought a book aimed at pet owners that you haven't – it is advised you wait until October/November before mating your doe(s) so that the babies will be born around spring time. This means that the weather will hopefully be better (depending on the country you live in of course) which is not only easier for travelling should you need assistance from an experienced vet but will also make it easier to raise the babies.

Buck Service

Right, you have a plan in place for after breeding and a registered doe suitable for the task. What you might not have is a buck but before you rush out to buy one you should look into buck service which is where you hire a buck from someone else. As mentioned earlier in the book it is not advised that you own an intact male as a pet and you should only buy one if you have four or five does that you want to breed.

Choose your buck very carefully. You want the babies to have all the strengths of your doe but none of her weaknesses therefore think about what you like most about your doe and what characteristics you would like to change then find a buck which has all of these qualities. For example, if you know your doe has a low milk supply and you want to increase this in the kids then choose a buck that is from strong milk goats and can correct this weakness in your own bloodline. If you want kids that have perfect show confirmation then look for a buck with this. Most owners who hire their bucks out will know about their bucks' strengths and weaknesses and if you approach them with your list they should be able to find one that is suitable for you.

Generally, most buck owners will only breed registered does which is another reason to only breed a registered goat. Generally, the bucks' owner will ask to see your goats' papers before they loan you the buck. They will most likely want to do a health inspection to ensure your doe is healthy and free from disease so don't be offended. In fact you should do the same with their buck. The bucks' owner may also want to know the does' history such as where does she come from, how long have you owned her and so on.

The rest is entirely down to you and the bucks' owner. Some owners may allow their buck to come to your property for breeding whilst others will prefer you to take your doe to them. There are pros and cons to each. For instance, if the buck is coming to you then this may be easier from your point of view because the owners should bring and collect them, however the downside of this is you then have to look after a buck for a couple days and all this entails such as the noise and the smell. Unless of course they bring their stud and just wait a few hours – the problem with this is that the goats may not breed immediately.

If your doe is going to the buck then you will be taking and collecting them. Many buck services will work this way because they will often be providing this service for those who own dairy farms and bring in two or three does at a time. In this instance you will need to be able to trust the owner enough to look after your doe but most people who offer buck service are farm owners and professional breeders who know what they're doing so I wouldn't worry too much as long as you have done your research on them and have got some references from other people who have used them if possible.

Buck service isn't usually that expensive. In the UK it costs around £50 and approximately £5 per day for boarding your doe. In the US it is around $50-$75 per doe. If you take your doe to the buck you usually get two visits included in this price. If you are boarding your doe then you may have to pay a few dollars boarding fee.

The downside to buck service is that there are laws that govern this now so you need to be clear about what these are and what you need to do to comply. In the UK you will need to speak to DEFRA or Trading Standards who will put you in touch with the right department.

The Breeding Process

Once you know your doe is in heat and you have found a suitable buck then breeding is really just a matter of putting the two together.

Usually the buck will start pawing and stomping to show that he's interested. If the doe urinates he may put his face in it. The pair may run around together for a while but then the doe will eventually start to wag her tail and stand still whilst she waits for the buck to mount her.

Some goats prefer to breed at night which is why it is better if you can board your doe or keep the buck on your property for a few days.

How Do I Know If My Doe Is In Heat?
Female Pygmy Goats go into heat throughout the year but it can be difficult to recognise this in the summer months, especially with younger goats, although these cycles should settle down and become more predictable as they get older. Adult females are in season approximately every three weeks and this can last anywhere between one and four days.

The best time to mate is day two or three. If possible, try to recognise when your doe is in heat and keep a diary of this for at least two or three cycles before you plan to breed her. This way you can be certain that she is in heat when you take her for buck service. Being in the presence of a male can trigger your doe to go into heat early so if you are taking her to buck service, knowing your doe's cycle means you can take her in a day or two before she comes into season which increases the chances of breeding being successful first time round.

Signs which indicate that your doe is in heat include tail wagging, mounting her goat companions or letting them mount her, clear discharge, increased urination or bleating for no apparent reason.

Sometimes does go into silent heat and don't show any symptoms so if you are going to use buck service and want to know if your doe is in heat you could use a buck rag which is a cloth that has been rubbed over the male goat so that his scent is transferred onto it. If you wave this buck rag under your female's nose and she shows interest then chances are she's in heat and it is a good time to put her with a male goat.

How Can I tell If My Doe Is Pregnant?
Pygmy Goats can often look pregnant all the time due to their naturally barrelled shape. Finding out if your doe is pregnant is usually just a matter of waiting. If you have kept a record of your doe's cycles then you can tell just by noticing if she comes into heat three weeks after being with a mate. This isn't always successful

however, because some females can still look like they are in season even if they are pregnant, although this is rare.

You may notice a change in your females personality a couple of weeks after being bred – friendly does may become more aloof whereas ones that were standoffish may become overly affectionate. This is due to a change in hormones.

Some does start putting on weight during the first few weeks of pregnancy so if your female does start to look bigger then she could be pregnant.

A urine test can be done fifty days or more after breeding and this is often a good indicator of whether your doe is pregnant or not. Your vet should also be able to do a blood test around this time to determine pregnancy.

You may decide to just observe your female after she has been mated and try to look for the signs yourself which is fine but it is recommended that you get her scanned at the vets at around six weeks into the pregnancy so that you can be certain that she is pregnant and can also find out how many kids she is going to give birth to which will help you determine her feed pattern for the final six weeks of pregnancy.

Gestation Period

The gestation period for Pygmy Goats is around 143-157 days on average. Anywhere within this length of time is considered normal.

Preparing For Birth

You should keep feeding your doe the same amount as before during the first part of her pregnancy and nothing else need be done until it is nearly time for her to give birth. If you are feeding your goats together make sure that the pregnant doe is getting her fair share and isn't being pushed out by the others in your herd. If necessary put her in her own feeding area.

To keep stress levels in the latter half of pregnancy to a minimum I would trim the female doe's hooves and give her a quick trim earlier on so that she will be comfortable during the birth, especially if the weather is warm. Once she's had the babies you will want to give her time to recover so doing all this grooming beforehand means you won't have to do it so soon afterwards. If the weather is cooler just clip their udder, belly, back of legs and under their tail area for hygiene reasons and to enable the goat to give birth and nurse without hair getting in the way.

At around three and a half months you can gradually start to increase her concentrate feed, but you should never give her more than double her normal amount. Quantity really depends on which type of feed you use and how many kids she is carrying.

A month before your female is due to give birth make sure she gets vaccinated as this will give the babies protection against Entero-toxaemia and Tetanus for the first eight weeks of their life.

Approximately two weeks before she is due you should provide your pregnant doe with a kidding stall in which to give birth. Make sure this area has been cleaned out and disinfected first and always ensure the doe has a clean, deep bed of straw.

By this time you should raise the water bucket off the floor so that the doe can just get her chin into it because newborns have been known to fall into water buckets and drown.

Watch your doe very closely around ten days before her due date just in case you see signs that she is ready to give birth sooner than expected. Pygmy Goats very rarely go up to the hundred and fifty day mark and it is not unusual for them to give birth at around day 145 or 147.

Physical signs that your doe is going to give birth include her udder filling up with colostrum, teats looking shiny and full and a slackening of the muscles on either side of her spine. You may notice that your pregnant female starts pawing at her bedding or is more vocal than normal, she may even turn her head and start bleating at her side.

Day Of The Birth

Ideally, as a pet owner, you should have a vet present when your goat gives birth unless you are an experienced breeder or an experienced goat farmer so I'm not going to go into the details of how to assist with a birth. What you can assist with is providing clean towels and cleaning their face and nostrils.

Many experienced breeders will say that you shouldn't be in a rush to take the kids and you should let the mother do her share of the cleaning and drying as it allows them to bond. Whilst I am inclined to agree, if the weather is cold or if the mother refuses to lick the sticky mucus off the babies then you should do it for her. The last thing you want is for the kids to become ill because they are cold. If there is more than one baby then you can be drying the first one with a towel and spraying it's cord whilst the mother is busy with the second then swap them over.

Once the kids have got the all clear you should clean up the bedding and provide fresh straw then give the female goat a drink of fresh warm water so she can replenish any fluids that were lost during birth. Some people add glucose or molasses to give the doe an energy boost but if she isn't used to this it can give them diarrhoea so don't go overboard with it.

Allow the kids to nurse and receive colostrum within twenty minutes of being born, as not only will this help settle them and allow them to bond with their mum but the colostrum will also provide antibodies to keep them healthy and help their immune systems. You should check to make sure that the kids have found their mum's udder, especially if it is the female's first birth as they often tend to back away when the kids approach that area. If necessary you can hold the mother whilst the newborns start to feed but the vet should give you advice on this.

Lastly you should watch out for the placenta, it may take several hours to come away but don't be tempted to pull on it, as this can cause damage. If it falls out whilst you are there then remove it immediately as the female can try to eat it and could choke on it.

After The Birth

Kidding can be stressful, which leaves does more susceptible to parasites so you should drench your female with a de-wormer a few days after they give birth. Make sure you check the label on the de-wormer to ensure it doesn't affect the milk and is safe for the kids to drink.

After four to five days you can give the newborn kids probiotics to help their rumens start working. This can be bought as a paste which you can squeeze onto your finger and place on the roof of the kids' mouths.

After 7-14 days your baby goats should be ready to disbud, with males being ready on the earlier side and does on the later side. You should start checking for horns early on, especially if you have bucks, as these tend to grow fairly quickly. Disbud them as soon as you can feel them if you are planning on getting rid of their horns.

At one week old you can start to milk your doe for your own benefits even if the kids are nursing. If you do this at around a week then this will ensure that your goat starts to produce more milk overall. You should milk in the morning then the kids can start to nurse throughout the day.

If you only have a single kid then check your female's udder because sometimes a lone kid can just feed from one side, which leaves the doe's udder uneven. If you milk the opposite side then you will actually be helping the doe out because otherwise it can be painful if the milk isn't removed.

If your doe is a freshener – that is she's never been bred or milked before – then doing a small milking session will get her used to this. It's not a 'full' milking if the kids are nursing as well so she won't have to be as patient but it will get her familiar to the routine and the milk stand and she will start to associate this with breakfast and treats, making it less stressful than if you just put her straight on the milk stand and take all her milk from her in one go.

At two weeks you should start to separate the kids from their mom at night. I would start this late in the beginning and give both the doe and the kids hay to nibble in order to distract them. Once they start to get used to it then you can separate a little bit earlier each night until eventually you are separating at dinner time.

It is important to consider whether you will be breeding before you build your barn so that you can have separate pens put in. Even though you are separating you can still keep your does and babies side by side with a fence between so they can still see and hear each other. I have seen barns which have separate pens but a shared metal hay rack so the goats are still eating together.

The reasons for separating are to get the goats used to being apart if you are selling but also so that the kids can nibble on their grain without their mother gobbling it all down.

Separating means you can go and play with the kids alone without their mother enabling you to bond without the doe interfering and allows you to bottle train them.

Another reason for separating is that you can milk the doe(s) in the morning without the kids running around or nursing before you get a chance to put your doe on the milking stand, once you have milked you can put the goats all together again.

By three weeks the kids should all be eating well and you should be able to milk more for your own use. Kids should be vaccinated with a CD/T shot and also given Di-methox 12.5% (sulmet or corid) to prevent coccidiosis.

By seven weeks your bucks and does should be separated full time. By this point you should put your bucks as far away from the females as possible to ensure that a baby doesn't impregnate other females in the herd, including its sisters or mother. You should be aware that separating with a fence may not be enough because there have been stories of bucks impregnating females through fences and whilst these tend to be older goats I would still err on the side of caution and keep them fully apart.

Bottle Or Dam Raise?

Dam raising means allowing your kids to nurse from their mother until they are fully weaned whereas bottle raising is just that – feeding your kids via a bottle of milk.

There are pros and cons to both. Dam raised kids tend to settle in the herd better and are more sociable with the other goats, whereas bottle fed kids tend to be off by themselves more.

If you are keeping your kids then you may prefer them to be closer to their herd but if you are planning on selling them then bottle raising may be best because it gets the kids used to people and stops them becoming too dependent on their mother.

Whichever you choose, handle each kid daily and spend time in the pens playing with them. Usually they will use you as a human climbing frame and will try to climb in your lap and over your back if you let them. This will enable them to be confident and sociable with humans which is what you want if your goats are to become good pets either for you or for someone else.

Weaning

By eight to twelve weeks your kids will be ready to wean and they should be eating plenty of grain and hay and grazing. By this point they will be ready to be on their own full time which is when you can start to send them off to their new homes if you are selling them.

Before they leave you, it is sensible to have them fully weaned at least a week before they go to their new owners, as this is less stressful for them – although if they have been bottle fed from an early age it shouldn't make too much difference – and also means you can detect any problems should they arise before they are sold. The last thing you want is for a kid to be returned because their new owner is saying you've sold them a sick or unhealthy goat.

Milking

If you are breeding your pet goat so that you can have milk then you should have lessons with an experienced owner who knows what they're doing in order to learn a good technique. This will not only be more productive because if you know what you are doing you will get more milk out and in a shorter time, also improving your goats mood as they won't be stood around for too long and it will also help to keep your goat healthy. You should always maintain high standards of hygiene so that you don't put your goat at risk of mastitis or get poor tasting milk.

Once you are milking for your own consumption and the kids are weaned then you should milk twice daily to keep your goat comfortable.

To maintain this milk supply you will need to breed your female once a year. Your doe can get pregnant whilst she is lactating and you can continue to milk your goat whilst she is pregnant however, you should stop milking at least a couple of months before she is due to deliver and allow her milk supply to dry up so that her body has time to rest and build up a good nutritional reserve ready for the new babies she will have. There is nothing wrong with breeding purely for a milk supply but please do so responsibly, your priority should be your doe's health.

Selling The Kids

You may be planning to keep your newborn Pygmy Goat but if you have two or three in one birth is this possible? It may not be realistic to keep them so please ensure that you are selling to good owners that understand how to look after these animals.

Remember that sudden dietary changes can make Pygmy Goats very ill so make sure you give information on what you have been feeding them as well as other general information on how to look after them. NEVER sell one goat to someone unless you know for certain they have another goat at their house. Remember these are herd animals and need to be kept in pairs. Some people will want to buy a lone goat either because they had a goat that died and need company for the remaining one or possibly because they are breeders that want to keep their bloodlines fresh but you need to be certain that these are the reasons for buying one goat and that you aren't selling to a novice who thinks they can just keep one as a pet.

Chapter 11: Training

When you think of Pygmy Goats it may not even cross your mind that you can train them but like dogs, there are many different things they can learn to do.

Goats are smart and just by repeating behaviour over and over will help them to pick up certain actions. For example, if you stand in the same place every day and give your goat a treat, eventually you will find them standing in that spot waiting for you because they associate it with a treat.

It is easier to train younger goats but just as you can teach an old dog new tricks so can you teach an older goat; it just takes a bit more time and patience. The younger you can train your goats the better but more important than age is having a trusting relationship.

Bottle fed kids are easier to train than those goats that were dam raised because they will already see you as the food giver and will most likely follow you around anyway. Again, it is not impossible to train a doe raised kid but you should build a bond first by taking them away from the other goats and spending time with them on your own until they are used to you.

If you have an aggressive or not very friendly or co-operative goat then the things listed below may not work for you. Like people, all goats are different and what works for one doesn't necessarily work for another – goat training can be fun though so it's always worth a try!

Food
You may have heard the saying "a way to a man's heart is through his stomach" and the same is true for goats; these animals will do pretty much anything if food is on offer, especially if it's something they really love.

My advice is before training find out which treats your goat particularly enjoys and use those for training. Examples include apple, second cut hay, raisins, small carrots, small pieces of garlic, small amounts of grain, banana peel, corn chips, animal crackers (for those in the USA) or other fruits and vegetables.

Patience

Your goat isn't instantly going to understand what you want them to do and you will need a LOT of patience when teaching your goat anything, even if it's just getting them used to the milk stand or walking them round on a leash. Rather than spending an hour or so on one trick and expecting them to learn it, the key is to show them what you want them to do, give them a treat, repeat the behavior and then let them go off and do whatever they want to and return later in the day to repeat the training.

Your goat may be in a piggish mood and not want to work with you – if this is the case rather than lose your temper simply stop, take a deep breath and try again. If they are still being stubborn then leave it and try again at another time.

Training should be fun for both you and your goat. Don't lose your temper and yell or hit your goat because this will make them nervous and less likely to trust you.

Basic Training

So you have food and you have patience, what can you teach your goat to do? Before you do any tricks you should give them basic training which is walking on a leash and standing at a milk stand or similiar.

Leash Training

If you are planning to attend shows then leash training is crucial because you will need to lead them around a ring so teaching them beforehand will make them easier to handle in front of a judge. Even if you don't want to attend any shows, leash training is still helpful as it makes it easier to move your goats from one place to another if you need to and will get them used to following simple commands.

Start by letting them get used to a collar – put one on and then give them a treat. If they seem happy with the collar on then add a leash and give a gentle tug.

Move slowly and don't pull too hard; you want to coax them to move but don't want to choke or strangle them. If your goat takes a few steps then give them a treat.

Repeat this for a few minutes each day, waiting until they take more and more steps each time until you give them a treat.

Milking Stand
As a pet owner you may not be breeding or milking your goat but you may use a milking stand or something similar to trim their hooves.

Whilst Pygmy Goats love to climb for some reason they are not too enamoured to be put in a milking stand so if you are going to be using one of these then start by walking them to the stand a few times a day just so they can see it, giving them a treat when they get there.

The best milking stands are those with a feeding bowl at the front; once they start to associate this with food they will begin to go willingly and eventually you should be able to coax them onto the stand.

Once you get them onto the stand, start getting them used to being touched by picking up their hooves if you are going to be hoof trimming. If you are planning to milk then start getting them used to you touching their udders. If your doe is already lactating then just do short milking sessions, little and often until she is used to it.

Soon they should be happy to get onto the stand and will eat their food whilst you are doing whatever it is you need to do. If this isn't the case and you find that even after training your goat still kicks out a lot then you may consider purchasing hobbles. These are canvas straps that fasten around the goats' legs with Velcro above the knee. The hobbles hold the goats' legs together which makes it harder for them to kick or buck although they may still be able to jump and move about.

Teaching The Word 'No'
Something I have found is that people think it's funny or cute when their goat runs at them and jumps. Whilst it is sweet when a baby goat jumps on your back you don't want a bigger goat charging at you (especially if you decide to keep the horns) so I would always start to teach them 'no' when it is doing something you don't want it to do. For example, if your goat starts to be pushy and shoves at you because it wants treats or if it steals food or is climbing on the fence, et cetera, you will need to teach them 'no'. Whilst it is fine to train your goat with treats it needs to learn that you give treats when they do certain behaviours and not just because they demand it.

As well as saying no move the goat away from whatever it is it's doing, so if it is near the fence say no and move it away, if it is pushing or jumping up at you then say no and firmly move it away. Another way to reinforce no is to squirt it with a water bottle.

If you are teaching no then correct the behaviour every time it displays it. Your goat will become confused if you let it climb on the fence some days and not others.

Fun Tricks
There are plenty of different tricks you can teach your goat once they have got used to leash training. This can include shaking hands or 'high fives', jumping through hoops, ringing bells, walking in and out of your legs, standing or walking on their back legs, walking across a balance beam or running an agility course. Whilst I've listed a few I'm sure there are plenty others that you could find to teach your goat but I think the principle is mainly the same for each.

These tricks can be taught in a variety of different ways; some people will use a clicker, others may use an animal training stick. My preference is with food and voice commands but if these don't work for you and your goats then you may find an alternative way that works better.

Standing On Hind Legs Or 'Dancing'
Choose a cue word such as 'stand' or 'dance' then say this clearly and firmly whilst holding a treat above your goat's head.

You may want to first hold the treat in front of your goat's face so that they take notice of it and then slowly lift it upwards and back in a straight line. Your goat should follow it until eventually they lift their front feet off the ground.

If they don't lift their front legs you can gently lift their front legs up for them the first few times to show your goat what you want them to do. As soon as they are on their hind legs, give them a treat. Repeat a couple of times then let them go off and do other goat things.

Once you've done this over several days your goat should start to anticipate the treat and stand on their back legs as soon as they hear the cue word. Once they've learnt this trick you can teach high five, sit and shaking hands in much the same way.

Jumping Through Hoops
Again choose a cue word such as 'jump' and hold out a hula hoop in front of your goat a little way off the ground. On the other side of the hoop hold out a treat and your goat should jump through the hoop to get it. Again, repeat daily until they can do this just by hearing the cue word.

If you want to add some pizazz to your trick you can add streamers to your hoop once they have got used to jumping through it on command or you can start to cover your hoop up with paper a bit at a time until there is just a small gap in the centre for them to jump through – eventually you should be able to cover this up with tissue paper or thin paper with the words 'ta da' written on it. As the goat jumps through, the paper will tear but it looks impressive to onlookers as they see your goat leap through a covered hoop!

Beam Walking
Goats tend to believe that the best way to get to what they want is to move in a straight line which is why they are fairly easy to train,

especially with tricks such as standing on hind legs, jumping through hoops and walking along beams.

To teach them to walk over a beam simply lead them up to the top of the beam then go and stand at the other end and place a treat. Make sure they see you do this. Your goat should simply walk across the beam to get the treat.

In the beginning if you prefer you could stand at the side of the beam a little way in front of them and hold the treat out, moving slowly so that they have to walk across the beam. Use a cue word so that eventually they will start to walk simply by hearing this word.

Ring A Bell
To teach this trick you want the goat to learn that when the bell rings it will get a treat so to start off just ring the bell yourself a couple of times, each time it rings give your goat a small treat.

If you want the goat to ring the bell with its head then hold the bell in front of the goat at head height and hold a treat right next to it. Choose a cue word such as "ring" or "ring bell" or "make noise" then wait for the goat to touch the bell with its head. As soon as it does this give them the treat even if you have to move the bell with your hand in order for it to ring. The main thing you want the goat to learn at this point is that the bell rings when they touch it. Repeat this a few times until you think your goat has understood the trick. Always give the command and hold the bell close until the goat understands the trick, then if you want to you can mount the bell on a post so that you don't have to hold it. You still need to make a fuss and give a treat as soon as the goat touches the bell.

If you want the goat to ring the bell with it's foot then you will need to teach it how to shake hands first. Hold the bell in front of the goat and give the command for shake hands followed by the cue for ringing the bell so this might be "shake and ring" or something. When the goat lifts its leg up for the shake hands command move the bell in front of its hoof so that it touches it then give lots of praise and a treat. Again, you may have to move the bell with your hand at the same time to get it to ring when the goat touches it. Repeat a few times then just give the command for ringing the bell once you think the goat has understood the trick.

Once you've repeated enough times that you think the goat has understood, move the bell a bit further away rather than directly by its head or leg. Give the command and the goat should move towards the bell and ring it.

Fetch An Object
You can teach your goat to bring you an object such as a handkerchief, tea towel, scarf or piece of cloth. Make sure the object you choose isn't too big or heavy for your goat to carry, a thinner material works better than a thick one. Whatever you use make sure you don't mind getting it dirty so don't use anything precious like your mum's favourite tablecloth.

This trick is a lot easier if you have a goat that tends to put stuff in its mouth anyway but even if you have one that doesn't often put anything in its mouth other than food you can still teach it.

First of all, put a few small treats in the centre of the material and hold it out in front of your goat. They should shove their nose in it and eat the treats. Repeat this a few times a day for a few days until your goat associates the material with treats.

After a few days of feeding treats from the cloth, hold it in front of your goat and give a cue word such as "fetch" or "bring cloth". If the goat puts its nose or mouth anywhere on the cloth give it praise and a treat. Repeat this again several times.

Eventually you should be able to give the cue word such as "fetch" and the goat should pick up the object and bring it to you – in return for a treat and lots of praise of course!

Tips
Whilst you probably want to train both your pet goats only train one goat at a time. Have a small area where you take each goat to train them. Whilst the other may watch and learn this way you want to make sure you are teaching them one on one otherwise you may find the goats just play and bond with each other rather than you. You

may choose to teach one goat a trick over a few days and then work with the other one or you may decide to spend a few minutes with each goat separately every day.

Keep your training sessions short. If you try and train them for hours at a time then not only will your goats get frustrated and bored but so will you. It is far better to have a few minutes repeated throughout the day.

Teach, treat, repeat – repetitiveness is the key to success, go over and over a trick several times a day and eventually your goats will understand what you want of them.

Always treat and praise your goat when it does something you want such as walking a beam, jumping through a hoop or ringing a bell, especially when it starts to do these things simply by hearing the cue words.

Don't reward bad behavior – if your goat is being pushy for a treat or jumping up at you don't give it to them. Just as you reinforce good behavior with a treat, if you treat bad behavior this will make the goat think it is doing something good. You may want to reward good behavior with a treat and discourage negative behavior by using a water bottle to give the misbehaving goat a squirt or two.

Keep your cue words different for each trick and try not to use similar words or ambiguous words like 'okay' as we often find ourselves saying words such as 'okay' for lots of different reasons and this can confuse your goat.

Try to bond with your goats before even attempting any training. If you have bottle fed kids then you are already bonding and well on your way to being able to train them but if you do have kids that were doe fed then rather than just going into their pen to feed and water them, hold their feed dishes and spend time in their enclosure with them to get them used to you being around.

Don't pull your goats – if you find they are not moving, for example, when you are leash training rather than pull them, try pushing gently from behind.

Conclusion

Pygmy Goats make such adorable pets; they're cute, playful and can be very friendly. Although they are increasing in popularity they are still quite unusual to find as a pet so if you are looking for an animal that is different from your ordinary dog or cat then these goats might be for you.

The concept of keeping a Pygmy Goat as a pet can be quite daunting if you have never had these animals before but as long as you do your research on what they eat and feed them the correct type of foods in the right amounts then you shouldn't have any problems. Understanding how their stomachs work is an important part of being able to keep them healthy. Remember to introduce new foods one at a time and over a period of time rather than all at once.

If you do purchase these goats they can be lots of fun. You can take them to shows or just train them to do tricks at home for your own amusement if you wish to do so. They are very smart and if you repeat things over and over they will soon grasp what you want them to do. Whilst there are a few tricks listed in this book there are also many more that you can teach them if you wished to do so.

My final thought on keeping Pygmy Goats is that although you will no doubt love them as a pet and maybe see them as no different to a cat or a dog, please remember that they are livestock and as such belong outside. Whilst they may come inside for a short while, it is far better for them to be outside with their other goat friends than inside with humans. They don't need to be tucked up in bed with you. They don't need to be dressed in clothes or coats no matter how cute they look! If you want to cuddle and play with them then do so in their own enclosure. This is for their own benefit as well as your own.

Printed in Great Britain
by Amazon

31536256R00066